Social Rehabilitation,
Care and Education
in Postmodern World

Social Rehabilitation, Care and Education in Postmodern World

Editors:

Anetta Jaworska, Danuta Apanel

impuls

Kraków 2009

Reviewer:
dr hab. prof. UG Mieczysław Ciosek

Cover design:
Ewa Beniak-Haremska

ISBN 978-83-7587-188-3

Oficyna Wydawnicza „Impuls"
30-619 Kraków, ul. Turniejowa 59/5
tel./fax: (12) 422 41 80, 422 59 47, 506 624 220
www.impulsoficyna.com.pl, e-mail: impuls@impulsoficyna.com.pl
Wydanie I, Kraków 2009

Contents

Part 2
Research report

|Introduction

An inherent part of the job of people who professionally help others is a constant search for solutions that enhance the human being's functioning in the world. Making the human world better is the only sensible aim of undertaking any social research. Supporting others in their maturation, development of potentials and the process of getting to know oneself and others are main messages of the theory and practice of education. The considerations presented in this book apart from educational problems include broader contexts of social reality, incorporating the area of care of the elderly and issues of social rehabilitation for the ones towards whom other educational measures have so far proved ineffective.

The first part of the book contains theoretical considerations about the contemporary social reality and the possibilities of carrying out constructive changes in it. Due to the fact that the increase of social pathologies and criminality is one of the dominant problems of the developing civilisation, the book begins with an article by Andrzej Bałandynowicz on the possibilities of increasing the rehabilitational effectiveness of punishments for criminals through the implementation of a widespread and consequent probation system. The author's considerations are not limited to criticising the present judicial and social situation. First and foremost, the author gives clear and concrete indications of the direction of the changes that should be undertaken in the Polish penal policy.

Consequently, a certain criticism of the present state of convict rehabilitation in Poland appears in the following article. The article describes legal acts that concern the execution of prison sentences and rehabilitation methods for convicts in penal institutions. An important part of this work is a description of certain paradoxes that are present in the penal policy and the reality of Polish prisons, among which the main one is the lack of rehabilitation possibilities and growing crime rates. Moreover, the article describes the specificity of rehabilitation of convicts that are addicted to alcohol and psychotropic substances and the conditions in prisons for the so called dangerous criminals. The author also points to the fact that there is a substantial underdevelopment within penal sanctions that constitute an alternative to the prison sentence.

When it comes to educational issues, Iwona Rudek describes educational programmes undertaken in schools. The aim of these considerations is drawing attention to the specfic character of programmes carried out by the teacher towards adolescents who require special competencies such as the ability to talk with the pupil.

Also, Wioletta Kopińska remains within the area of education in schools. Her considerations open the second part of this book that contains reports from social research. The presented studies underscore certain problems of the contemporary student governments. The author blaims lack of democracy in schools for the majority of the problems.

Renata Miszczuk in her article focuses on presenting care, education and prevention activities for children and families, people left on the margin in terms of rehabilitation and reeducation, the addicted and the co-addicted and people in danger of getting addicted to psychoactive substances.

The article by Agnieszka Próchniak depicts interesting studies on the attitudes of students towards cheating which they treat as an unfair method of competing with one another at school.

Joanna Nawrocka in her article discusses issues connected with taking care of the elderly. She presents the pilot study to a vast study on the social reception of senility.

Piotr Próchniak's two articles allow to draw interesting conclusions about risky behaviour of people that display prosocial attitude (firemen) and antisocial attitude (criminals).

The ultimate article concerns the area of criminality and the possibilities of convict rehabilitation trough the prism of research on the effectiveness of alternative support rehabilitation programmes in penal institutions based on yoga.

The other articles also pertain to the areas of education, care and social rehabilitation. It seems that this book can become a source of new questions and quests in the field of science but, first and foremost, educational, care and rehabilitational practice.

Anetta Jaworska

Part 1

Theoretical background

Andrzej Bałandynowicz

Probation system – penalties of medium force and measures of supervised liberty as a proposal of fair punishment

The policy of punishing – weak points

In order to improve the efficiency of the measures of influence with regard to the perpetrators of incriminated acts they should be properly differentiated. The limitation of these measures to the punishment of imprisonment or probation measures is insufficient. At the moment there is an empty gap between prison isolation and standard probation. This gap can be bridged through punitive measures of a different kind.

The excesses in neither the liberalization nor the punition of penal measures are uncalled for. Therefore we need to grow more confident about the modification of probation activities milder than the penalty of deprivation of liberty. At present too many convicts are held in penal institutions and too few are subject to other measures of compulsory social control. On the one hand we tend to be too lenient in punishing, on the other – too severe. We are too lenient with regard to persons who should be under stricter social supervision and who are now subject to probation measures, whereas we are too severe with regard to those convicts who pose no serious threat to public safety.

Why does punishing policy fail to yield satisfying results? One reason could be social attitude to the measures of penal repression and the origin of the criminal law. Other reasons could be the unstable development of penitentiary structures or the multiplicity of institutions shaping the legal and the actual situation of persons penalized. In order to stimulate and improve the punishing policy, intermediate penalties, situated in between imprisonment and standard probation measures, should be introduced.

Why the term 'intermediate penalties' instead of 'alternative penalties' or 'alternative sanctions'? The term 'alternative penalties' implies some substitute of imprisonment, which may as a result suggest that imprisonment itself is the most effective form of punishment. On the other hand, the use of the phrase 'alternative' may become some sort of a promise of decongestion in penitentiary units, a promise that in present conditions cannot be kept.

We can expect that penalties like heavy fine, compulsory social labour, residential supervision or mandatory treatment would be applied, in the beginning at least, exclusively to persons either conditionally released from a part of imprisonment sentence or those with suspended punishment.

In order to bridge the gap between unconditional imprisonment and the actions undertaken in the case of probation, a system of intermediate penalties, appropriate for our present circumstances, should be designed and implemented.

Why intermediate penalties cannot be called intermediate sanctions? Whereas in social reception punishment is tantamount to imprisonment, intermediate sanctions would be associated with a slightly more lenient form of action taken against an offender who violated law. Intermediate penalties cannot thus become something extraordinary and less severe. They need to constitute a separate element of the system of measures of penal repression within their own right.

The punishment should be inevitable. The offender cannot escape suffering, constraint and liberty restrictions. The reduction of freedom rights may, however, take place not only in the conditions of prison isolation but also within the context of some social interaction of a different kind.

Nevertheless, it needs to be stressed that any offence against law should result in tough sanctions, for example imprisonment or intermediate penalties. None of the following is eligible here:
- capital punishment, which is not aimed at the offender's reformation and fulfils only the eliminating function;
- stigmatizing penalty, which causes disgrace;
- corporal punishment (e.g. flogging), which brings disgrace not so much to the offender but rather to the society advocating it.

The humble collection of probation measures (conditional release from serving the full sentence, conditional stay of the carrying out of a sentence and conditional discontinuance of legal proceedings) in operation in Poland at the moment does not allow to successfully eliminate the negative consequences of imprisonment and at the same time prevent from recidivism.

For some offenders the very fact of formal accusation or a record in court files may be a sufficient penalty. For others it is the procedures involved in the court trial and the fees paid to lawyers. The uncertainty and fear connected with the act of accusation and sentencing can be so harsh that frequently the sentence of punishment (without the ability of probation) becomes too high a burden for the offender.

How to differentiate between a properly formed and adjudicated intermediate sentence and standard probation? In some cases it can be very difficult. However, it is possible. Namely house arrest can be treated as both one of the conditions of probation and as a penalty of isolation established by an authorized institution. Intermediate penalties comprise: so-called intensive probation, financial penalties, compulsory social labour and other penalties, which are in fact ways of tighter control of persons sentenced in the conditions of restricted liberty.

'Intensive probation' is a term general enough to comprise a collection of restrictions infringing personal freedom within a community and a variety of programmes designed with a view to preventing recidivism. Subjecting the offender to a particular probation programme is a penalty of specific character, enabling precise examination and at least partial elimination of pathological factors, which may influence the perpetration of a prohibited act to a greater or lesser extent. The programmes designed to tackle the problems of drug and alcohol use as well as mental illnesses belong here. Intensive probation is house arrest (residential) accompanied in some cases by electronic monitoring. As a result the convict's supervision becomes more effective and crime control more successful.

Other intermediate penalties comprise: financial penalty (arbitrary fine) and compulsory social labour. The former is underestimated in Poland due to poor chances of its effective enforcement and nonegalitarian character. The latter has undoubtedly high educational qualities and helps to reinstate the offender in society.

Intermediate penalties should not function in isolation one from another. Financial penalty can well be combined with house arrest or compulsory social labour, which could additionally be supported by electronic monitoring. However, if this turns out to be insufficient, this collection of penalties should be supported with a short residence in a closed institution.

What system of intermediate penalties should be designed and implemented in order to avoid the accusation of granting privilege to some groups of offenders and dividing people into 'better' and 'worse' (the former go to prison, the latter are subject to intermediate penalties)? In what way should we control court rulings with regard to their appropriateness in order to minimize the incongruity of the punishment to the offence. In the future we will not be able to ignore addressing these questions. Perhaps we should address them now.

The offenders sentenced to arbitrary fine could additionally be subjected to the following:
- the order to recompense the losses suffered by the victim of the crime,
- full coverage of legal expenses,
- house arrest combined with electronic monitoring, the cost whereof would be met by the offender.

With regard to some categories of people violating law intensive probation could prove adequate. It would consist of the following elements:
- precise and regular supervision conducted by a probation officer or a professionally instructed policeman;

– temporary residence in a rehabilitation centre (e.g. for alcohol addicts),

– a commitment to work a set number of hours as social labour.

All the elements of intermediate penalties, however, need to be carefully executed. The ruling of an intermediate penalty serves a positive purpose not only for the offender but also for the victim of the crime and the society as a whole. As a result this method is economically superior to imprisonment.

The approval of this expanded system of punishments may prove rather complicated at the level of court sentencing. However, the expectations connected with it are concerned with a punishment commensurate to the social menace created by the offender as well as his or her personal characteristics. Reasonable penal repression should contribute to the abatement of the negative phenomenon of committing the crime again and greater flexibility with regard to court rulings.

Intermediate penalties should be integrated with the existing comprehensive system of penal measures. Penal policy can be executed effectively only if the total of penalties is supplemented with penalties adjusted to varied types of offences and different categories of offenders, on condition that these sanctions can be easily executed.

At present both theorists and practitioners in the field stress the problem of significant overpopulation in prisons and detention houses, as well as the ineffectiveness of the conditional release from serving the full sentence and the suspended sentence as standard probation measures. As a result we should no longer give preference to imprisonment as a principal penalty. At the same time the decisions of lenient probation measures are taken too frequently. Thus we should focus on a form of punishment combining harsh repressions with supervision at large; these conditions are undoubtedly fulfilled by intermediate penalties.

Until now the institutionalization of the system of penalties situated in between imprisonment and standard probation has not been accomplished. Imprisonment, being a principal penalty, has recently been applied only sparingly. In addition, it fails to provide a sufficient number of possible solutions. The selection, plausible in the future, between those rightfully sentenced to imprisonment and those for whom an intermediate penalty has been adjudicated, cannot be entirely based on the gravity of the committed crime or the frequency of the occurrence of the specific criminal act in a particular area. Similar criteria should also not be taken into account with regard to the choice between probation measures and intermediate penalties.

Intermediate penalties

The introduction of intermediate penalties to the system of principal penalties involves the necessity to confront a certain type of belief that criminal acts of equal gravity, as well as persons of similar criminal record, should be treated the same. It is a faulty understanding of the idea of appropriate punishment. Modern system of penal measures allows the adjudication of varied penalties in similar circumstances. As a result some convicts are sent to closed penitentiary institutions while others are subject to repressions at liberty.

What should be done in order that intermediate penalties can fulfill their functions?

Firstly, they need to be applied on a large scale, which would allow to eliminate the overpopulation of prisons and lead to gradual decrease in importance of both the institution of conditional release from serving the full sentence and suspended sentences of imprisonment.

Secondly, they need to be firmly executed. Dismissals and adjournments would be applied only in exceptional cases.

Thirdly, if the person sentenced to intermediate penalty fails to fulfill its requirements, the original repressions should be tightened relative to the offence.

Fourthly, fine, applied as intermediate penalty, should be considered as either a separate penalty or a part of a specified collection of sanctions. Only after the settlement of this matter should we establish the sum of money to be paid as well as the possibility of paying it in instalments. The amount of money to be paid should be adjusted to the financial capability of the offender. The dates of payments should be tightly observed. However, it is the way of estimating and the procedure of execution of payments that require the greatest innovations. At present fines are too low, they are not commensurate with the financial capabilities of offenders, and they are executed with difficulties.

Fifthly, compulsory social labour might be applied as either a single repression or a part of a collection of penalties. It might be adjudicated with regard to offenders of both high and low financial status. Its adaptation can bring positive results on condition that its execution is carefully supervised.

Sixthly, in order to achieve a significantly greater control over the behaviour of the persons sentenced within society and to enable their return to normal life, free from pathological phenomena, we should apply intensive probation, which can for instance combine house arrest with compulsory treatment and electronic monitoring (the cost of which would in part or in whole be covered by the criminal).

Seventhly, prior to the introduction of a new system of intermediate penalties courts should be subjected to the influence of specific interpretative directives of modern jurisdiction policy:

a) there is a whole array of cases in which the sentences of imprisonment as well as intermediate penalties might be applied to the same extent (similarly the probation measures and intermediate penalties);

b) a comprehensive collection of information about the offender should be compiled (his personal qualities, financial status, family relations, etc.) in order to be capable of deciding on an appropriate fine, compulsory social labour, treatment programme, residential supervision or monitoring with electronic devices, or the infliction of punishment of imprisonment and intermediate penalty as constituent parts of the same sentence (however, the two forms of punishment could not be executed simultaneously);

c) in the case when the person sentenced to an intermediate penalty fails to fulfill its requirements, the judge should tighten the sanctions, or even replace them with the punishment of imprisonment.

Eighthly, the effectiveness of the influence of intermediate penalties should be assessed very critically so that these measures are not considered euphorically the most appropriate instruments of penal repression.

For instance, 21 1941 persons were sentenced to imprisonment in Poland in 1999. Of this number 12 8561 persons had their sentences conditionally suspended. It is up to discussion how many of them could be subjected to intermediate penalties. Probably this number would be extremely high.

Should all the persons sentenced to imprisonment be subjected to this sanction? Defining the criteria justifying the decision to pass the sentence of the penalty of isolation from society might be an attempt to address this issue.

The sentence of stay in penal institution is reasonable only when the following criteria are met:

– any milder punishment would be incommensurate with the gravity of the committed crime (crimes);
– isolation from society would prevent any further violations of the law;
– milder repressions, applied previously, did not fulfill their goals.

Therefore, the punishment of imprisonment should be restricted to the cases when a heavy crime has been committed and there is a need to stop the criminal from perpetrating new crimes, and when other sanctions proved insufficient.

Applying only these criteria it might be stated that there are many sentenced persons who should not stay in prison. This group comprises persons committing not serious crimes and having short criminal records, who do not deserve to be separated from their families and friends. It is hard to estimate how numerous this group is.

In practice there is one reason which speaks in favour of the punishment of imprisonment. Even when the judge passing the sentence is skeptical about its possibility of reclaiming the criminal and deterring potential criminals from committing an offence, he or she is certain about one thing: staying in a penitentiary unit, the offender will certainly not commit any crime (except when on a pass). Preventing from further crimes is playing an increasingly important role in passing sentences and may in part explain the present overpopulation of prisons.

The preventive function of the punishment of imprisonment is to a large extent promoted for populist reasons, since courts anyway apply conditional release from serving the full sentence. Theoretically eligible for such release are prisoners who pose the least possible threat of committing a crime in the future, or at least during probation. In practice the procedure is rather automatic – the release is granted after having served a certain part of the sentence.

There are numerous prisoners in penitentiary units who are unlikely to violate the law in the future. Their only chance is conditional release from serving the full sentence. They need not stay in isolation from society since they pose no threat to it. On the contrary, they might prove useful to it. Many offenders belonging in this group could have been spared imprisonment if a properly advanced system of penalty measures existed.

On the other hand many convicts who have had their sentences conditionally suspended or have been granted conditional release from serving the full sentence should, while on probation, be subjected to supervision stricter than at present. For some of them, instead of suspending the execution of the punishment of isolation, an obligatory increase of the fine would prove more fitting. Others could for instance be assigned to different tasks connected with environment protection. The probation measures provided for in the present penal code fail to give the offender a sufficient opportunity of returning to normal life due to their mildness. The violation of the conditions of probation is frequent since its execution is not properly supervised.

To sum it up, the Polish penal code has not been sufficiently polarized. The kind of sentence passed of tentimes does not correspond with the gravity of committed crime as well as the threat the offender poses to the society. Between the punishment of imprisonment and probation measures there exists a gap, which cannot be bridged only through the penalty of restricted liberty. A comprehensive system of penal repression should be supplemented with a collection of intermediate penalties. This would help eliminate the punishment of imprisonment and probation measures with regard to certain categories of offenders.

In the period of the transformation of the political system we are particularly subject to the epidemic of crimes by so-called 'white-collars' as well as organized crime. In order to prevent these unwelcome social phenomena from happening, we introduce stricter laws concerning penal liability, mostly by increasing the threat of imprisonment with regard to specific types of offences. However, we fail to make proper use of the possibilities offered by financial penalty for example. Some countries, including Scandinavian countries, treat fine as a principal penalty in the system of penal measures. The amount to be paid is established on the basis of the convict's financial status and his or her earnings. It is a repression that successfully prevents potential criminals from violating the law. This is due to the fact that this penalty painfully diminishes the economic position of the offender. In Poland it is usually only a supplement to the punishment of imprisonment.

At present in Poland fine is calculated on the basis of the number of daily rates and the sum of money attributed to each rate. The minimum rate equals 10 zlotys while the maximum has been set at 2000 zlotys; the minimum number of rates is

10 whereas the maximum is 360. According to these specifications a minimum fine can be established at 100 zlotys while the maximum can amount to 720 000 zlotys. In addition to that, when passing a particularly aggravated sentence, there exists a possibility of the increase of the maximum number of rates to 540 which in effect translates to the fine of 1 080 000 zlotys.

The second aggravation of penalty in the context of financial penalty refers to certain crimes against economic turnover (art. 296 § 3 of penal code – abuse of confidence and causing damage on a great scale; art. 297 § 1 of penal code – money laundering). In these cases the maximum number of daily rates has been increased to 2000 – it applies only to a fine administered together with the penalty of imprisonment and equals 4 000 000 zlotys (Penal Code, Dziennik Ustaw No. 88/1997, item 553).

It needs to be stressed that in penal revenue law there has been introduced the rule of administering a fine on the basis of the number of daily rates and the sum of money attributed to each rate. The minimum number of rates is 10, the maximum – 720 (Penal Revenue Code, Dziennik Ustaw No. 83/1999, item 930).

Fines are underestimated as an penal instrument against more serious criminals. Financial penalties are perceived as inefficient with regard to persons of high financial status. At the same time they are not administered to pauperized individuals, forgetting that at the basis of the problem there is inefficient execution of the fine.

Fine, being a principal repression in the system of penal measures should correspond with the gravity of the committed crime and financial capability of the convict. More successful execution of financial liabilities can be achieved very cheaply if local governments and commercial financial instruments (e.g. banks) are incorporated into the system of executive authorities. Lacking appropriate funding and overburdened with work, courts are not effective executive bodies. This is the reason for disbelief in fine as a basic reaction to serious violation of the law.

I agree that fine is not an appropriate penalty for offenders with very low income. Adjudicated with regard to people lacking private wealth and means of survival, it becomes in reality tantamount to the punishment of imprisonment (substitutive penalty). Should all the pauperized offenders end up in prisons? Should they not be granted a chance of rehabilitation at large? Such possibility arises with social labour, which helps correct caused damages or contribute to the common interest in some other way. There is a noticeable impasse in house building industry; there is a lot to be done in the field of environment protection and municipal infrastructure. Should we not utilize the abilities and work of some convicts? The benefits would be multiple: the convicts would not stay in prisons (they could be lodged in dormitories) and would receive full board, the commune could benefit from cheap manpower, and the national budget would make savings. In the case of neglect of labour duties the penalty of compulsory social labour would be replaced with imprisonment.

Intermediate penalties also comprise other socially approved actions, among others intensive probation performed in all sorts of educational institutions as well as institutions for discontinuation treatment, or even in the convicts' places of residence (house arrest) – in this last case they would be supported with electronic or telephone monitoring.

It needs to be realized that many criminals require a stricter supervision than is the case with standard probation. However, it should not be so intensive as to conduct it through closing the offender in a penitentiary unit. Intermediate penalties seem to be an indispensable tool in the evolution of the measures of penal repression.

Advanced system of criminal responsibility

The funding for an experimental programme of intermediate penalties will surely be available. New initiatives always arouse vivid interest. However, the initial interest quickly wanes when comparisons are made with alternative solutions in the existing system. Will intermediate penalties face the same fate? Will we still be satisfied with the results in the form of a great number of projects that never come to fruition? It is hard to say. Therefore, let the efficiency be the final determining factor. Let us find out if the new system of sanctions succeeds in eliminating from prisons the less dangerous criminals, thus providing them with a chance of rehabilitation at large. I do not want the enthusiasm of reformers to dissipate in the red tape inertia.

We need to take a risk and overcome organizational, political and financial difficulties if we want new ideas institutionalized and the expected benefits achieved. It is absolutely obligatory that the funding for the implementation of the system of intermediate penalties be secured. Otherwise, the intensification of crime, and as a result the overpopulation of prisons, will become a standard.

If at some point the funding for the development of intermediate penalties is limited, there may occur a situation resembling that in the United States in the sixties. There was reached a breakthrough, or so it seemed at least, in the treatment of the mentally ill. Antipsychotic drugs enjoyed great popularity. There even appeared a social movement whose supporters advocated the reinstatement of the mentally ill into society. It was believed that mentally ill persons can work in groups (under close supervision of course), that they can be treated in clinics, where they would pay only occasional visits, and that they can stay at large in specially dedicated buildings. Unfortunately, antipsychotic drugs proved too expensive and the locations for occupational therapy, as well as dedicated clinics and centers for persons suffering mental diseases were not built in sufficient number. Hospitals were vacated, yet nothing was offered instead. Intermediate penalties are under similar threat. Their introduction into the system of principal penalties requires alterations in the system, and not only half-measures in the form of poor funding for project work and experimentation. Another half-measure would be the incorporation of the intermediate penalties into the existing system of penalties.

A system of a differentiated repression scale, from probation measures to the penalties of 'medium force' to the punishment of imprisonment will in effect be less expensive than that in which imprisonment is a dominating penalty. However, only on condition that an appropriate period of time has passed since the implementation of the reform. The great amount of work and funds will not yield instantaneous results.

The officials supervising the execution of intermediate penalties will be scarce in the beginning, which means that only a small number of convicts could be subjected to the influence of these penalties. The movement advocating 'alternatives to the punishment of imprisonment' has been set on the false premise of immediate savings. It has been forgotten that the budget of the system of prison organization can be radically decreased only if the number of prisoners diminishes in numbers high enough to close some penal institution or at least one of its units.

There is one more aspect that needs to be paid particular attention to: intermediate penalties must be rigorously executed. The criminal – drug addict who breaches discontinuation treatment programme needs to realize that he is now facing a penalty much more severe than the one originally adjudicated – a stay in a penitentiary unit.

In the case of financial penalty, commensurate with the convict's financial capabilities and with a set date of its payment, the most important matter is a simple and effective execution mechanism. The realization of the inevitability of the fine is of utmost importance since the number of fines, which have not been executed is significant.

In order to achieve the goals of intermediate penalties a consistent action needs to be taken, aimed at the schooling of professionals and the betterment of the efficiency of the executive apparatus.

It is my hope that in the next few years the position of the punishment of imprisonment as a principal penalty will be upset. Hopefully there will exist a system which will ensure the possibility of choosing one or a few penal measures (without the division into 'better' and 'worse' ones) for specific groups of criminals. Probation measures should be supplemented with intermediate penalties, assuming that probation measures will include only conditional release from serving the full sentence, suspended sentence of imprisonment and conditional discontinuance of legal proceedings. Creating a whole array of penalties enables the exchange of originally ruled sentence (even in the course of serving it) for a different one, if sufficient argumentation for such alteration is presented. The assessment of the gravity of the reasons for the exchange of one repression for another one (other ones) should be conducted by the court, which decision is taken on the basis of the opinion issued by the executive body.

These theoretical considerations may seem rather idealistic; however, they are a continuation of the achievements of the science of criminal law with regard to the fullest possible application of the rules of humanitarianism during the execution of penalties. Their introduction requires radical reforms in the field of sentence adjudication.

The situation in which the judge faces the actual choice between the punishment of imprisonment (or a fine) and conditional suspension of its execution must be eliminated. Otherwise petty criminals, persons socially maladjusted, and frequently persons disregarding the obligation to pay alimony are directed to prisons. The only chance they have is conditional release from serving the full sentence, possible to apply only after serving a part of the sentence and having a positive criminological prognosis. As a result they stand no chance of reha-bilitation, which might prove useful to the society. Legislative alterations which would shift the temporal restrictions regarding conditional release would be well worth introducing. An alternative solution might be the possible replacement of the punishment of imprisonment in the course of its execution with some other penalty, e.g. a fine or compulsory social labour. In this case a short-term impris-onment punishment would satisfactorily fulfill its function as a deterrent, while substitutive penalty would become an economic equivalent of damages and harm done to the victim of the crime and the society as a whole.

The proposals presented above would of course be subjected to appropriate modeling so that the broadest possible circle of convicts could regain freedom. Such opportunity would be refused for dangerous criminals, deeply demoralised offenders, and those who misused this chance in the past, if only once.

How then should a rational system of ruling sentences be designed?

Firstly, the principle of possible alteration of the sentence in the course of its execution must be accepted.

Secondly, the simplifications of the type 'either imprisonment or nothing (or almost nothing) must be avoided.

Thirdly, judges must be granted greater flexibility with regard to the choice of a penalty and sentencing.

The following classification of offenders would be a restriction:
– 'must be sentenced to the penalty of imprisonment'
– 'should be sentenced to the penalty of imprisonment, unless...'
– 'should not be sentenced to the penalty of imprisonment, unless...'
– 'must be sentenced to a penalty other than the penalty of imprisonment'.

The above classification categories have been constructed on the basis of two equal criteria: the gravity of committed crime and the offender's criminal record.

Fourthly, the choice of an appropriate penalty should be left entirely within the court's jurisdiction.

The system of measures of penal repression, supplemented with a collection of intermediate penalties, may face heavy criticism on the part of judges and all the advocates of equal treatment of offenders who have committed the same crime. Obviously a situation may occur when two criminals who committed crimes of equal gravity are treated differently. One of them can be granted a milder penalty – a fine or compulsory social labour, whereas the other – the punishment of imprisonment.

The accusation of unfair treatment, however, can easily be refuted. Is it not commonplace now that judges differ in their appraisals, ruling varied sentences of imprisonment for offences on the same scale of punishment? The advanced theory of penalty requires the acceptance of the fact that the sentence adjudicated is an individual case and needs not be repeated precisely in following sentences with regard to offenders in the same category. The only thing that can be established in this field is the approximate equivalence of penalties for a specific type of crime.

The consequence of the introduction of intermediate penalties to the system of penal measures would be the shift of a significant number of offenders who would otherwise stay in prison to the sphere of compulsory social influence in the conditions of personal liberty. The offender benefits from such situation by staying at large; society benefits for economic reasons. On the other hand, the number of persons subjected to probation would decrease; intermediate penalties can successfully replace, for instance, sentences of imprisonment with conditionally suspended execution or conditional release from serving the full sentence (in this case a part of the imprisonment of punishment would be replaced with, for example, a penalty of compulsory social labour or house arrest).

The court, balancing in the sentence the degree of violation of particular interest protected by law and the type and severity of sanctions, should pay more attention to the objectives of specific types of punishments and decide on a punishment which either eliminates the criminal from the community (the punishment of imprisonment) or reinstates the offender into the community (intermediate penalty). Dangerous and demoralized criminals, who will never adjust to 'normal life' should be isolated from the society for as long as it seems rational.

It needs to be understood that it might prove very difficult to convince judges that the penalty of imprisonment is just one of many penal repressions and that it should not be applied too frequently. In my opinion the Supreme Court should play an important role with regard to the new Criminal Codification. Its authority may influence the policy of judges with regard to the rational choice of penal sanctions, including imprisonment.

Of practical difficulties, accompanying the incorporation of intermediate penalties into the system of measures of penal repression, the most difficult seems to be overcoming stereotypical thinking that the penalty of imprisonment will remain the punishment for pauperized persons, while persons of high financial status will be subjected to other types of penalties.

Let us consider this on the example of two criminals addicted to drugs and accused of banditry. Either of them has already been sentenced for similar crimes. Both are majors of the same age. The criminal A is a student, comes from a complete family, depends financially on his parents, belongs to the middle class and on a number of occasions has been subjected to expensive discontinuation treatment programmes covered by the family. The criminal B comes from a pathological family, with many children, in very difficult living conditions, depends financially on temporary social benefits and cannot afford any discontinuation treatment.

The criminal B should be placed in prison, since no alternative sanction could be applied here:
– a fine would not be paid;
– compulsory social labour would be out of the question due to drug addiction;
– supervision in the conditions of intensive probation would be illusory
– the cost of compulsory treatment in discontinuation treatment centers at liberty would have to be covered by the state while the criminal, suffering no financial liabilities, would in fact be 'awarded' for the criminal act. Therefore in this case drug treatment should be administered in a penitentiary unit so that the penalty could have some impact on him. He needs to understand that the penalty of imprisonment is a chance for him not only to fight the addiction but also the possibility of this penalty to be replaced in the future with the penalty of compulsory social labour.

The procedure with regard to the criminal A should be different. Instead of sentencing him for imprisonment, the judge could rule a financial penalty, which would be a form of compensation for the damages and harm caused for the victim of the crime as well as for the society. Thereafter he should be subjected to intensive probation supervision (one of the conditions of probation would be regular participation in the discontinuation treatment programme, the cost of which would be covered by the criminal; additionally he would be regularly subjected to tests for the presence of intoxicants in the organism). His stay at large would be organized in the conditions of house arrest and, if necessary, supervision with electronic devices (the convict might be obliged to meet the cost of the device).

Insisting on the placement of the criminal A in prison only because there is a lack of sufficient funding to deal with the criminal B at large, is an example of illusory aspiration to equality in physical suffering and at the same time a perfect means of overpopulating prisons. If we continue to treat the penalty of imprisonment instrumentally as a dominating sanction we do not only refuse a chance to the criminal A, but also make impossible the successful treatment and return to a normal life of the criminal B.

The offenders who are capable of rehabilitation at large and who do not need to be socially isolated should not be placed in penitentiary units. Their 'freeing', however paradoxically it may sound, will be beneficial to these criminals, who either must be placed in prison or need to stay there due to the fact that no alternative penalties are appropriate for them. Reduced prison population can be subjected to much more intensive therapeutic and reformatory treatment, which is the objective of modern penitentiary policy.

A comprehensive system of reinstating criminals into society, based on probation measures, intermediate penalties and the penalty of imprisonment, is very flexible. This should not be forgotten by courts when choosing a collection of sanctions for a particular offender.

A good penal system is one, in which penalties are equal with regard to criminals committing the same type of crime and having similar criminal records. However, we need to consider in what sense they should be equal. There are at least two planes on which this equality might be found.

From the criminal's point of view the equivalent of the prohibited act is being subjected to suffering or appropriate sentence of imprisonment. Courts, however, should have a different notion of equivalence – as the sum of functions performed by penalties, frequently of different types with regard to criminals of similar types.

The penalty of imprisonment comprises varied forms of suffering, varied types of the intensiveness of the suffering as well as different scopes of infringement of personal liberty. Nevertheless it can easily be noticed that differences in the status of prisoners and the difference in types of penal institutions exclude any equivalence. However, only in the eyes of lay persons is imprisonment for one year an equivalent of rational punishing policy. Such judgment stems from the notion of penal justice obtained from popular sources rather than from thorough professional publications in the field of criminal policy. The impact of the majority of society is so strong that legislative bodies frequently yield to the magic of the most severe punishments, and restricts the authority of courts to sentencing and administering penalties that are invariable, unquestionable and quasi-egalitarian. Equality in suffering and infringing freedom rights is an illusory ideal – a wrong understanding of the rule of common equality. Penalties should not be differentiated into severe and mild, but into appropriate or inappropriate with regard to the character of the incriminated act. Their equivalence should be measured against the expected outcome in the form of the correction of the damages of the crime and proper compensation, rehabilitation or isolation from society. Only this kind of approach, free from excessive strictness, enables the acceptance of intermediate penalties as measures equivalent to the punishment of imprisonment. Only when we have realized that this 'inequality' is a false notion, can the problem be overcome.

The interest of many social groups is restricted only to the most serious, the most sensational, or the most brutal crimes. The great majority of these cases do not qualify for intermediate penalties. The publicity these cases receive results in the lack of social acceptance for the differentiation of penal sanctions. This in turn reinforces the dominating position of the penalty of isolation as a kind of remedy for the threat of crime. The institutionalization of intermediate penalties will not be possible unless the majority of society, still believing that harsher penalties reduce crime, accepts them.

Pain and suffering can determine condign punishment only in the sense that repression neither depreciates the gravity of the crime and the criminal record of the offender through, among others, the understanding of his or her present situation, nor sanctions suffering excessive with regard to the committed act or the degree of the criminal's demoralization. However, this does not exclude the possibility of applying the penalty of imprisonment with reference to some criminals, whereas others would be subjected to intermediate penalties for similar behaviour.

Is the degree of the restriction of autonomy a better measure of the equivalence of penalties than pain and suffering? The restriction of liberty as a result of imprisonment is obviously significantly greater than in the case of house arrest combined with electronic monitoring. However, if we were to assess the rightness of each single case of ruling a specific penal sanction, we would need take into account both social and individual cost-effectiveness of this particular sanction. The cost of staying in penal institutions is a burden to the state, while the expenses connected with the purchase and management of the electronic device is covered by the convict.

The person staying in prison, on the one hand, 'uses' social welfare, on the other hand, is forced to resign himself or herself to the regime of the state. The person subjected to house arrest, on the one hand, enjoys more freedom in his or her personal life, on the other hand, is forced to meet the very high economic cost of the adjudicated penalty. The lengths of residential supervision and imprisonment can be balanced so that house arrest is an equally severe punishment as imprisonment. To accomplish this, a revolution in the way of thinking about just penalty needs to be conducted, which seems to be real in the foreseeable future.

Thus the idea that just and equal penalty is, for instance, the sanction of five years' imprisonment, can in reality be subject to different modifications in the eyes of the offenders themselves. Some will consider it positively as a form of free board and accommodation or as an opportunity to meet persons from criminal circles, others – as the deprivation of the chance to recompense to the society and the victim of the crime for the damages caused or as a period of mere frustration and humiliation.

The full equivalence of penalties remains an ideal which needs to be pursued. The type of penalty and sentencing should not depend on subjective social expectations but rather on an objective assessment of the potential effects of punishment.

Let us consider this thesis on a specific example. Two offenders have committed a crime of the same type, e.g. a burglary. Both are drug addicts. Let us assume that both wanted to steal objects of comparative value and both have previously been convinced. The criminal A has no professional education, is unemployed, lives in very bad conditions, in a family with many children, and makes a living from social benefits and occasional physical work. The criminal B has a steady occupation, has graduated from a high school, has no financial problems and has good living conditions in his parents' house. Would the following penalties be just for them? For the criminal A – two years' imprisonment; in the course of serving the sentence in a penitentiary unit he would participate in a discontinuation treatment programme and afterwards, when he is released from prison, he would undergo treatment in a specialized centre, covered by the state. For the criminal B – three years of intensive probation on the following conditions:
 – one year in discontinuation treatment hospital (closed institution),
 – the following two years – the obligation to contact the probation officer and regular tests for the presence of intoxicants in the organism; in addition to that he would be obliged to fix the damages of his crime; the cost of discontinuation treatment and the expenses connected with the probation supervision would be covered be the convict.

Such differentiation of sanctions seems reasonable from the perspective of functions they can fulfill with regard to society and the offender himself. The support on the part of family, proper education and the possibility of the continuation of employment at liberty cannot be disregarded when deciding on a penalty (a collection of penalties). Should we continue to advocate the thesis that for both the criminal A and the criminal B the most appropriate penalty is imprisonment, which embodies the faulty notion of common equality before the law?

Insisting on both prisoners being sentenced to imprisonment only because no penalty, other than imprisonment, considering his difficult social situation, can be applied to the criminal A, is nothing but an attempt to achieve the seeming equality for an excessive price. Neither the criminal A, nor the criminal B, nor the society would benefit from it. Criminal law is incapable of righting the social inequalities. However, this leads to some sort of moral inequality, which necessitates the consideration whether the system of differentiated penalties will be socially accepted as just, and whether it can function properly.

The belief that the evaluation of sanctions on the basis of pain, suffering or the restriction of autonomy, has no significance, and that the equivalence of penalties should depend on their functions, should prevail in the criminal policy.

The interpretative directive explaining the need of understanding equivalence as a result of function fulfilled by the penalty, should become the principal argument in sentencing, and choosing a specific form of penalty, by judges.

If the objective of the punishment is to deter the offender from a second offence, it can be achieved with similar results by either a short-term imprisonment, or a properly high fine. Similarly, the isolation function can be equally successfully fulfilled by either prison or house arrest combined with electronic monitoring.

Benefits achieved through financial savings and the elimination of unnecessary suffering speak in favour of less restrictive intermediate penalties, the functional objectives of which are entirely different from the objectives of the penalty of imprisonment.

The theory of condign punishment

When we say that a penalty is condign we mean that it is neither too severe nor too mild; it is also neither adequate to the criminal's subjectivity nor proportional to the degree of harmfulness of the criminal act; nor is it a penalty so cruel that the offender is deprived of a chance to return to normal life. A condign punishment is a just punishment, far from both excessive rigour and abolitionism.

The dialectics of human thought and actions will in time determine the minimum and the maximum of condign penalties with reference to specific types of crimes or offenders of similar nature. Such values undoubtedly exist; however, their pursuit requires patience and resistance to the pressure of public opinion, which invariably tips the scales of justice in favour of excessive rigour.

Determining the maximum and minimum penalty which can be ruled with regard to a specific type of crime, the legislator often succumbs to emotions, perceiving criminals exclusively as persons demoralized, socially maladjusted and not deserving being given even a single chance of rehabilitation at large. Not all of them, however, are dangerous; many of them have been pushed to crime by social and financial situation, the lack of knowledge of the law, or simply an accident. The worst thing is that practically the only alternative to the sentence of imprisonment (without the ability of probation) is the reduction of the length of time in prison.

Associating just penalty only with the temporal dimension of stay in a penitentiary unit has to raise objections of criminal law theorists. Even greater objections should be raised against the stereotypical thinking in the form of the acceptance of the rule of application and execution of the penalty of imprisonment as a guarantee of the convicts' equality in suffering and the restriction of autonomy. If this solution were to be adopted, we would face the necessity of the creation of new penal institutions and the developments of those already existing. In such a system few convicts could hope for a penalty other than imprisonment.

An alternative to this is a modified system, which needs to be introduced in order to avoid excessive strictness in criminal policy and penitentiary policy. For serious crimes the punishment of imprisonment is ruled, for less serious ones – other sanctions, e.g. fines, compulsory social labour or probation supervision. In general offences against life and health should be addressed in the form of repressions of isolation, while offences against property and economic offences should be addressed through economic sanctions, often very harsh.

However, even the system 'the penalty of imprisonment or other penalty plus the equality in suffering or autonomy restriction' would be excessively strict due to the difficulties with proper assessment of economic and moral damages with reference to specific types of crimes. The division into groups would most probably be conducted on the basis of the rule of 'the worst case', which could lead to the paradox, where a bandit who stole an insignificant sum of money with the threat of violence, would be treated by court much stricter than an embezzler who misappropriated billions from the national budget. Legislative authorities, determining the limits for a given crime, adjust them to the most brutal cases of the violations of the law. This puts at a disadvantage 'average' offenders, who become 'victims' of the rigourous attitude of the legislator, almost by accident. If we want to introduce a system of reasonable and just punishment, we need to reject the schematic thinking when sentencing. The decision which penal measure to choose and how best to administer it for a specific offender should fall within the jurisdiction of courts. In consequence the most repressive penal measures will be applied more sparingly.

One more aspect, very important and frequently disregarded, needs to be stressed – internal modifications within particular offences. The punishment of imprisonment can be executed differently depending on the type of penal institution and type of programme applied. The lightening of the effects of a penalty may, for example, be accomplished through frequent granting of permits or the possibility of employment outside of prison. The shortening of the period of isolation in prison, in the form of conditional release from serving the full sentence, can also in a way differentiate prisoners. As far as the financial penalty is concerned, its modifications could comprise postponement of payment or the payment in installments. I think that a new instrument, applied in particular circumstances, should be considered for the introduction to the punishment execution code – the reduction of a part of the total payment (the frequency of ruling the substitutive penalty of imprisonment would decrease).

In the case of the penalty of intensive probation appropriate fulfilling of the duties and careful observation of the conditions of close supervision should signal the possibility of their temporal reduction. The same should be true for the penalty of compulsory social labour.

There is a whole array of possible solutions with regard to the formation of obligation and the ways of supervision in the case of intensive probation, as well as the kind and frequency of tasks in the case of compulsory social labour. Skilful use of the internal differentiation of penalties can become the most effective instrument of eliminating punition from the existing penal system.

In conclusion I would like to say that the dominating position of the penalty of imprisonment in the collection of principal penalties, though persists, has received crushing criticism. At present the punishment of imprisonment is no longer considered as a corrective measure; in addition, there are many voices pinpointing the steady dehumanization of prisoners in the conditions of prison isolation. The pursuit for a just system of legal repression, based on physical and mental suffering connected with imprisonment, should be rejected in a democratic country, where the preservation of human rights is not merely declarative.

The introduction of a new system of criminal responsibility, based on intermediate penalties, is hampered by complications of legal, political, ideological, organizational, and financial nature.

Legal barriers are connected with the difficulties of adapting the institution of intermediate penalties – as a product of Anglo-American legal systems – to Polish legal landscape (penal code, code of penal proceedings, punishment execution code). The foundation of a new system of sanctions might be the following: the penalty of restriction of liberty, the fine, security measures (isolation and treatment), probation measures (conditional discontinuance of penal proceedings, conditional release from serving the full sentence) as well as the institution of the exchange of a penalty for a less strict measure. In order to conduct a thorough reform of the penal system, it does not suffice to exchange old institutions with a few new ones. First, we need to diagnose the reasons for the malfunctioning of previous solutions. Only then should we introduce new instruments of the policy of punishing or modify the ones existing today. The greatest obstacle to the introduction of the system of intermediate penalties in Poland seems to still be the propenitentiary character of the regulations of the criminal substantive law (the statutory sanctions regarding regulations contained in the special section of the penal code), law of criminal proceedings (the role of temporary arrest – preventive measure of isolation in the legal proceeding), and criminal executive law (in the punishment execution code the penalty of imprisonment occupies the central and dominating position).

A superficial analysis may support the belief that it is sufficient to introduce changes in penal codifications aiming at the reduction of the rank of the institutions of isolation, and thus effect changes in the collection of principal penalties in the form of more humanitarian measures. This type of rationalization is unsatisfactory since from the very beginning arise complications, among others of practical nature.

The introduction of amendments of legal acts of statutory rank requires the will of political parties holding the majority in the parliament. Without the support of influential politicians no legislative initiative will survive through the legislative process.

The inability to convince the parliamentary majority (political obstacles) may result in the situation where the revolutionary changes in criminal policy regarding the introduction of intermediate penalties will never reach out behind the sphere of analytical studies.

Political barriers closely correlate with ideological complications. Numerous politicians, drawing on fossilized theories of penalty and interpretative stereotypes rooted in common social conscience, promote populist ideas on the sources of crime, restrictive methods of reacting to it, and positive or negative effects of particular penal repressions. This ideology of social justice clearly leads towards a punitive penal system, with the penalty of imprisonment and the capital punishment being the most effective sanctions. Therefore the stress put on the insufficient sense of certainty of the authorities and the insufficient sense of legal safety of citizens, and the connected notion of the ways of controlling crime, do not pave the way for the modifications of the system of penal responsibility by means of introducing a catalogue of intermediate sanctions.

Apart from this, the introduction of new penal/legal reactions creates, in the beginning at least, numerous structural and organizational problems. Subjects responsible for carrying out decisions taken in penal proceedings are then subject to reorganization involving retraining of the personnel to new tasks and the rotation of persons not fit for fulfilling new professional functions. Changes of this kind are never positively received by the personnel responsible for the execution of penal measures. The incorporation of intermediate penalties to the system of principal penalties and as a result partial elimination of the penalty of imprisonment would be most painfully felt by prison staff. Their position would be weakened in favour of the bodies executing financial liabilities, probation officers and policemen. Therefore the most significant force opposing the new system of sanctions seems to be the present organizational structure responsible for the process of the execution of the penalty of imprisonment.

The transformation of many penitentiary units into social rehabilitation centers or discontinuation treatment centers, the rationalization of the system of the execution of financial liabilities, as well as the retraining of probation officers and police personnel, requires also appropriate financial resources. Thus, complications of financial nature can be the next obstacle in the reformation of the penal system towards its rehumanisation. National budget, burdened with both external and internal debt, excessively in the field of expenses, is not able to participate in the cost of the reform aiming at the incorporation of intermediate penalties to the system of principal penalties. The cost of this operation would have to be met by communes. In the first place, however, they would have to be convinced that investments in executive infrastructure with reference to intermediate penalties would be profitable to them. The potential profits would comprise the acquisition of considerable group of convicts for physical work (the penalty of compulsory social labour) and increased receipts (paid discontinuation treatment, the execution of financial liabilities and other types of fees connected with the execution of supervision in the conditions of intensive probation.

The long list of obstacles standing in the way of the alteration of the penal law does not mean that the introduction of these modifications will be impossible. However, an appropriate strategy, able to overcome these complications, will have to be created. Changes in social policy dealing with the forms of crime control should begin with the reformation of social attitudes, influencing public opinion and the legislative authorities as well as numerous opponents of the proposed reform. The leading argument of this campaign would be the necessity of creating a modern and effective penal policy of crime restriction.

Intermediate penalties cannot be perceived as an alternative to the punishment of imprisonment. They are independent sanctions, bridging the empty gap between the stay in prison and probation measures. The system of responsibility, in which the penalty of imprisonment is considered as a principal penalty, and other measures as its mere substitutes, should be a thing of the past as quickly as possible. This is the opinion of not only the representatives of the world of science of criminal law, but also judges and prosecutors, who perceive the overpopulation of penitentiary units and the degradation of reclaiming programmes as a very dangerous social phenomenon. They all see the need to modify the existing system of penal responsibility and are potential supporters of intermediate penalties.

Is the reform aiming at the introduction of a new type of sanctions to the collection of principal penalties profitable in the economic, political and legal sense?

In the first stage of the introduction of the reform – investments – the political and economic cost of the introduced changes can be quite high while the effects – insignificant. We cannot expect, in the short term, a sudden reversal in the tendencies in sentencing policy of courts or a radical decrease of the number of prisoners. This requires considerable time.

At the beginning intermediate penalties would fulfill the role of aggravated probation measures. They would probably replace the penalty with conditionally suspended execution of sentence, conditional discontinuance of legal proceedings, and conditional release from serving the full sentence (in this case there would be possible an alternative in the form of a punishment of imprisonment plus an intermediate penalty). Such a solution would be the most appropriate for both subjective and objective reasons. Subjective would be those which are connected with the irresistible will of judges to rule severe repressions and thus pandering to the public opinion (e.g. conditional suspension of the execution of sentence is socially perceived as a measure too mild and inadequate to the damage and harm inflicted. On the part of objective reasons would be the quickest possible transformation of the base organizing social interaction in the conditions of probation into an infrastructure indispensable for the most efficient use of the collection of intermediate penalties.

In order to prevent a total depreciation of the institution of probation measures and exchanging them for the penalties of: compulsory social work, house arrest or fine, we need to create, as quickly as possible, a situation when intermediate penalties are adjudicated with regard to criminals who should not be directed to penal institutions (or should no longer stay there) and who at the same time do not deserve the chance of returning to society in the conditions of standard probation.

The cost of departure from the system based on the dominating position of the penalty of imprisonment can be so high, however, that intermediate penalties will never counterbalance the penalty of imprisonment and will not result in the decrease of the number of prisoners. The lowering of these expenses is, nevertheless, possible on the condition that thorough modification of the existing system is quickly and efficiently executed as part of detailed restructuring programmes, in which there would participate not only state-run units, but also communes, banks and other subjects, e.g. insurance companies or social organizations.

Firstly – the programme of restructuring and development of penitentiary infrastructure. Centres of social rehabilitation and discontinuation treatment, run on the principle of partial or full cost coverage, as well as dormitories for those sentenced to compulsory social work, could be created on the basis of eliminated penitentiary units. The majority of prison personnel would be employed in these institutions.

Secondly – a programme of retraining a part of prison personnel to the execution of new tasks involved in the supervision of persons subjected to house arrest (training in the use of electronic monitoring devices).

Thirdly – a programme of more efficient execution of financial liabilities. Fines could more successfully be executed if this task is redirected to the executive bodies of banks, insurance companies or local government units.

Introducing communal and commercial bodies as a part of the system of execution of penal measures leads not only to the restriction of the extent of the application of the penalty of unconditional imprisonment, but also to the acknowledgement of the rules of procedural justice and compensatory justice as principal and determining directives of modern punishing policy.

Summary

Effective, from the perspective of social security, substitutes of the penalty of imprisonment have been investigated worldwide for decades. Recently there has been an increased interest in the search for so-called 'third way' in the system of legal consequences of committing a crime. It focuses on such repressions applied to the offender which can in effect bring 'reasonable' benefits both to the society and the victim of the crime. A system of modern criminal policy incorporating intermediate penalties and probation sanction, designed by the author of this work, is a manifestation of these investigations. It is a novelty with regard to the existing system of penal norms and to the changes proposed in the projects of legal legislation. The principal objective of this reform is the alteration of the way of thinking of practitioners in the field. We need to reject the idea that a crime of equal gravity and persons of similar criminal record have to be treated equally. We need to discard this way of understanding of the principle of condign punishment once and for all.

Anetta
Jaworska

Organization of prison management in Poland

Introduction

The most common notion assumed to stand for the social rehabilitation of convicts in penal institutions is rehabilitation. The notion refers
specifically to the Polish reality and brings negative connotations in Western
European countries and the U.S.A. Thus, it needs to be stated that the notion
of rehabilitation encapsulates all activities of educational character, trainings of
skills and therapies that are undertaken in penal institutions in order to prevent
reoffendering.

The Polish system of penal policy is maladjusted to the changes in criminality taking place at present in Poland. This dysfunctionality is the result of i.a. an
general escalation of criminality and an appearance of new types of crimes after
year 1989 (the year of the fell of communism and the beginning of rapid social
and economic changes in Poland) such as organised and international crime.
Members of organised crime constitute at present 3,4% of all imprisoned and
detained in Polish prisons (2845 prisoners) whereas there were only a few people
some years back.

The statistics of the Central Committee of Penal Services state that there
were 84 609, including 2592 women, prisoners on the 31st of January 2009 in
all penal institutions of the country. Due to lack of places in the overcrowded
penal institutions there are 38 713 that await the execution of the sentence and
2498 are at present exercising the right to suspend the execution of the sentence.
The overcrowding of the penal institutions is the most noticeable sign of the
dysfunctionality of the Polish penal system. However, there is also a low level of
effectiveness of social rehabilitation of the people that leave the penal institutions
and a high level of reoffendering. The opinions on the Polish penal system are
beginning to be more and more critical and contribute to the general crisis of this
type of convict rehabilitation.

Legal basis for penal actions in Poland

According to the Polish penal executive code (The act from 6th June 1997) social rehabilitation of convicts in penal institutions is a right of the convict and not a duty. Thus, it constitutes a voluntary offer presented to the convict which s/he can accept or reject. A system of programmes is obligatory only for juveniles (prisoners of 17–21 years of age). The rest participates in the programmes only if they agree to. In the article 67, paragraph 1 of the penal executive code (PeC) the legislator states that the aim of activities in the penal institutions is to stir in the convict a willingness to cooperate in shaping a socially accepted attitude in them, especially one of responsibility and a need to perceive the legal order and thus refraining from reoffending. The article also describes the ways of penal rehabilitation that is an individual action towards the convicts within the framework of the systems of punishment execution in the different types of penal institutions as determined in the article (Lelental, 2001). Social rehabilitation in the penal institutions is mainly carried out by means given in article 67, paragraph 3 of the PeC :
- work (particularly if aimed at obtaining appropriate professional qualifications),
- teaching,
- cultural and educational activities,
- sport,
- maintaining contact with family and the external world,
- therapeutical means.

Many of the methods of actions used in the Polish penal institutions have not been taken into consideration in the Polish criminal law. However, the legal acts do not state precisely which methods can be used in resocialisation in prisons. The corrective possibilities of the contemporary prison spur many controversies. According to the research on reoffending of R. Martison (1974) carried out almost 40 years ago, there are no significant differences between people who took part in action programmes and those that did not participate in any resocialisation programmes. Also in present conditions, despite the emergence of new forms of resocialisation work in the penal institutions, a major part of the society and also – which is particularly sad- a major part of practitioners – does not believe in the rehabilitational effectiveness of the prison. The process of punishment execution in the conditions of prison isolation prisonises rather than resocialises by stigmatizing the convict as a criminal both during and after the execution of the sentence. Furthermore, it develops an attitude of claiming and learned helplessness.

Among the methods of penal actions practiced not included in the PeC but nevertheless practiced in Poland, there are the following forms of working with convicts:

- methods based on personal influence (i.a. the authority of the educator, educatory counseling, convincing, conversation);
- religious activities in prison – all the convicts have a possibility to benefit from the service of a priest and even make pilgrimages to places of religious cult. The prison chaplain often performs the role of an 'unpaid' educator in a penal institution);
- cultural activity in the society (prison theatres and musical bands that perform i.a. in nursing homes for the elderly and even in kindergartens);
- work with the disabled (helping in daily activities and helping disabled children in learning swimming or horse riding);
- work in hospices with the terminally ill;
- various types of training groups;
- methods based on culture (such as artistic work – annual exhibitions and competitions of prison art, sculpture, painting, poetry) (Jaworska, 2008);
- a certain novelty is the interest in methods based on the ecological activisation of prisoners – prisoners take part in i.a. the annual 'clean the world' programme that consists in cleaning the streets but also forests and river banks. They also work with animals in shelters or learn ecological methods of plant cultivation (e.g. in the 'Black sheep' programme);
- apart from the well-known and generally accepted methods there are alternative methods such as yoga ('Prison Smart' programme based on the assumptions of yoga that functions in 52 penal institutions in Poland) and music therapy by means of using music bowls (so called Tibetan bowls) led by a prison warden in a penal institution in Wierzchowo Pomorskie.

In the recent years there has been an increase in the programmes realized in the Polish penal system. Among the programmes realized in the penal institutions there are: cultural and citizenship education programmes; aggression and violence prevention programmes; alcohol prevention programmes; drug addiction prevention programmes; HIV/AIDS prevention programmes; health promotion programmes; professional activation programmes; programmes on physical education and sport. The programmes are rarely rooted in the theory and reflect the results of empirical research to an insufficient degree. Among the few programmes based on empirical evidence there is a world-known Aggression Substitution Programme, therapeutical programmes and the presently implemented programme for the resocialisation of sexual criminals. The majority of other programmes are new proposals prepared by psychologists and educators employed in penal institutions. According to A. Majcherczyk (2006, p. 34):

> Colleagues from western countries after the presentation of our system are very often impressed by how much we have managed to achieve. However, the first question is usually about the effectiveness of our programmes to which we usually give a diplomatic answer that we are currently working on it, whereas we should rather say

that we live in a little bit different world. We do not think about measuring effects. We are happy if we manage to carry out any programme at all...

The implementation of new programmes into the Polish prisons is truly satisfactory when one takes into consideration the fact that 18 years ago the main form of social rehabilitation work with the convicts was... a talk.

PeC from 1997 defines a model of punishment execution that underscores personality factors of the prisoner and introduces a subjective treatment of the prisoner. However, in the search for effective rehabilitation methods one needs to concentrate not only on the convicts' personality but also on providing them with optimal conditions for the process of reintroduction to society. It is these specific conditions that influence the shape and structure of the convicts' personality.

The organization of the penal system in Poland

There are four major types of penal institutions in Poland (Act from 6th of June 1997 art. 69 of the PeC): for juvenile delinquents, for first-timers, for reoffenders and for people in military custody. The penal institutions can be organised as: closed penal institutions, half-open penal institutions and open penal institutions. 70% of the existing institutions are closed (Szczepaniak, 2003, p. 49).

They differ mainly in the degree of security level, the isolation of the convicts and the duties and rights of the convicts in terms of moving around the institution and beyond it (art. 70). The prison sentence is executed in the system of action, therapeutic and normal programmes (art. 81).

In Polish penal institutions the majority of cells are double cells – 26,1%, 3 person cells constitute 14,4%, whereas 19,2% are 5 person cells. Overcrowding in the penal institutions results in a systematic increase of the number of cells with many inmates and the number of beds in the existing big cells (Szczepaniak, p. 104).

The Polish endeavours to become a member of the European Union (membership since 1st May 2004) allowed to use the means of non-returnable financial help offered by the European Union to candidating countries in order to equalize economic differences. Also, the prisons profited from the EU help programmes. By means of using the EU structural funds the Polish penal system received a chance to implement new means of carrying out rehabilitation with the inmates and to develop a system of support. In practice, there is an increase in the level of debts of the penal institutions which means that the search for saving is more important than the rehabilitation of inmates who one has to dress and feed and also patch a leaking roof.

Prison buildings are usually situated on a small area and isolated from the rest of the world by means of walls and barbed wire above which there are watchtowers. This is how a border between the place of isolation and the area of the free world is created. The fact that most of the prison buildings are very old has a negative influence on these conditions. More than 70% of the buildings were built before World War II and have not been remodeled or modernized since, whereas 96 out of 156 penal institutions and custody (64,5%) were built before World War I (Bulenda, Musidłowski, 2002, 21). There are also facilities from the 17th and 18th century, however, the oldest buildings still in service, e.g. in Barczewo, Łęczyca and Koronowo are from 13th and 14th century.

The characteristics of inmates in Poland

The vast majority of the population of convicts in Poland is characterized by alcohol abuse or addiction to alcohol. The disorders are sometimes very serious and result in cirrhosis or alcoholic epilepsy. A vast majority of the convicts are emaciated people that do not care about their health or appearance. There are mainly people with very low level of education, mostly with elementary education. About 2/3 of the convicts did not have a permanent job before getting into prison, often remaining unemployed due to their own choice. About 8% of the convicts in penal institutions (Malec, 2006) are people sentenced for misdemeanor and not felony who end up in prison as a result of not paying the sentenced fine. Some of them are put in prison only for a couple of days. The usual misdemeanors are: small scale theft committed due to poverty, drinking alcohol in a public place or disorderly conduct. They are sentenced to a substitution punishment in prison because they do not have the money to pay the fine. It should be asserted that such individuals are in want of social support, health and sanitation help – but this should not be the task of the penal institutions. Such a stay in a prison that lasts a couple of days does not fulfill either a correctional or a deterring function – yet, burdens the penal system to a significant degree.

Penal rehabilitation of addicted convicts

A spreading drug addiction in the penal institutions is a particular hindrance to rehabilitation. Until the beginnings of the 90s the most popular drug was the so called 'tchay' (which began being used among the convicts sentenced to prison after World War II in Soviet concentration camps) which is a very strong intoxicating tea infusion drank by the prisoners. The custom is cultivated only by a small number of reoffenders and does not gain popularity among the younger inmates (Dubiel, A. Majcherczyk, 2006). At present, it is marihuana and amphetamine that constitute the real problem. However, anabolic steroids, Ecstasy and heroin are also used to a great extent.

An up-to-date therapeutic base for addicted convicts in penal institutions comprises 33 wards, including 20 therapeutic wards for alcohol addicts and 13 wards for drug addicts and abusers of psychotropic substances. The number of places in the therapeutic wards is not sufficient to cater for the needs. The convicts wait about 10 months to be accepted to such a ward. Actually, the extent of addiction from psychoactive substances is so huge that each penal institution should have their own therapeutic ward. The programmes carried out on therapeutic wards are rarely adapted to prisoners, that is, they are not developed for people who remain in prison. The programmes are developed mainly by means of transferring the methods used with addicts who are not criminals to penal institutions. Programmes used on addiction wards are short and usually last around 12 weeks. Prolonging them is usually not possible due to a high number of convicts who await their turn to take part in the programme. A good aspect of the Polish system of addicted convict therapies worth underscoring is applying systemic solutions, installing the therapy within the structure of penal institutions and aiming at incorporating all the addicted convicts into the programmes. Perhaps an increase in the staff and the therapeutic wards would be possible if a major part of the prison finances was not given to the the wards for the so called dangerous criminals that are half empty.

Penal rehabilitation of dangerous criminals

According to the Polish Penal executive Code prisoners commonly called 'dangerous' are describes as: constituting a serious danger to the society or the penal institution. According to article no. 88a & 2 of the PeC such a convict: 1) has carried out an attack on the independence and integrity of the Republic of Poland, the political system or the life of the president of Poland; committed malice murder, took or held a hostage, hijacked a ship or plane, committed a crime in possession of firearm or explosive material or 2) was an organizer or an active participant of a group uprising; assaulted an officer or another member of prison staff; raped or maltreated an inmate; escaped or tried to free somebody from a closed penal institution or during escorting.

An accepted solution for the rehabilitation of groups of dangerous convicts is placing them in specially designed housing units in closed penal institutions. There 16 such departments In Poland at present, however, almost half of them remains empty. The number of dangerous prisoners has remained unchanged in the recent years. There were 346 of them on the 31st of January 2009 (Central Board of the Penal Service). The Polish legislation places dangerous criminals under strict isolation in prison. They are even stricter than for life sentence (currently there are 238 prisoners in Poland with a life sentence).

Creating separate housing units for dangerous prisoners is the outcome of the idea of multilevel isolation of different intensity. The cells of dangerous prisoners remain locked round the clock and are monitored (after the 3 recent suicides of dangerous prisoners one after another, full monitoring of the cell including the sanitary corner). Such convicts will be able to work and learn exclusively within the unit they are held. Thus, dangerous criminals are confined to small areas, sometimes for many years, with extra safety devices (within other security measures of the closed institution), with constant monitoring and frequent control procedures. The law does not define either the minimal or maximal period for the status of a dangerous criminal – this is a decision of the penal commission. In practice this often signifies that a convict can have the status of dangerous even throughout the whole period of isolation. In the conditions of far reaching isolation the possibilities of any educational influence on the convict are severely limited. In practice, the convict remains alone in the cell round the clock and cannot participate in group activities, learn or work. The convict has few possibilities to show that they do not pose a social threat any longer. The only indicator is their behaviour throughout the execution of the punishment. Moreover, there is no law that prohibits going out of prison after doing the sentence – directly from the unit for dangerous criminals.

Discussion

A heated discussion led in Poland proves that the Polish criminal law is to lenient in comparison with world and European tendencies, though not so long ago – in the 80s it was accused of unusual severity. Nevertheless, it seems that the Polish criminal law and justice remain quite severe which can be illustrated by the fact that the main sentence in the Polish courts is a prison sentence. A deficiency in punishments alternative to prison sentence is observable. The weakness of the probation system manifests itself i.a. in a small range of community service type punishments, a marginal use of mediation and difficulties in enforcement of fines (which is characteristic of poor societies) and consequently changing it into a prison sentence. Thus, the Polish criminal law remains almost as severe as during the times of Soviet influence in Poland – before 1989, though the conditions of punishment execution have improved significantly and can be accepted in a legitimate system of justice. The visible severity of the criminal law does not bring about a decrease in crime. It is quite the opposite. The tendency seems contrary to the one observed in the USA (Murray, 1997) where crime was on a rise until the imprisonment coefficient and the related risk of a prison sentence were on a decrease. When the situation reversed and the risk of imprisonment increased – crime started to decrease. The analysis of American literature (Zimring 2007) suggests that crime reduction was brought about also by other factors than severe criminal law and a higher risk of a prison sentence. It could probably be claimed that crime would be decreasing in the USA even if there was an increase of the severity of criminal law. The influence of the severity of criminal law on the level of crime should thus not be exaggerated and treated in absolute terms as crime rates are determined by many factors. If the severity of criminal law and repressive conditions of punishment execution had such enormous influence on fighting crime, many Eastern European countries (such as Russia) and other countries that remain under the influence of communist ideology that use drastic methods of treating the inmates should already be countries with no crime at all (Krajewski, 2008). The American model in which there is a positive correlation between tighter penal restrictions and a decrease of crime rates seems unusual from the European point of view (Great Britain, Germany, Holland, France, the Czech Republic, Hungary), including Poland where the crime rates increase rather than decrease if the number of prison sentence is higher. In European countries, where there is a reduction of the number of inmates, e.g. in Finland, there is no sudden increase in crime rates as it is related to a number of factors and seems to be influenced mainly by economic stability and a stable social and political system. Meanwhile, making penal restriction more severe and building new prisons seems a major idea to reduce crime in Poland. However, prison sentences do not diminish but rather increase social problems (Andrews, Zinger, Hode, 1990). A prison sentence during which there is no inmate rehabilitation programme does not decrease but increase reoffending which is observable also in Poland.

References

Andrews D. A., Zinger I., Hode R. D., *Classification for effective rehabilitation: Rediscovering psychology*, 'Criminal Justice and Behavior' 1990, 17, 19–52.

Bulenda T., Musidłowski R. (ed.), *The treatment of prisoners 1989/2002*, The Institute of Public Affairs, Warszawa 2002, 21.

Dubiel K., Majcherczyk A., *The Polish therapy system for drug addicted convicts*, „Przegląd Więziennictwa Polskiego" 2006, 52–53, 51–72.

Jaworska A., *The readaptive value of arts in penal institutions*, Słupsk 2008.

Krajewski K., *The extent and dynamice of the prison population in Poland in comparison with European tendencies. Comments on two contentious issues*, „Przegląd Więziennictwa Polskiego" 2008, 37–54.

Lelental S., *The penal executive code. A commentary*, Warsaw 2001.

Majcherczyk A., *Programmes for the resocialisation of convicts – a voice in the discussion on the state and perspectives of the penal system*, „Przegląd Więziennictwa Polskiego" 2006, 52–53.

Malec J., *Prison sentence for misdemeanour convicts*, „Przegląd Więziennictwa Polskiego" 2006, 52–53.

Martison R., *What works? Questions and answers about prison reform*, 'The Public Interest' 1974.

Murray Ch., *Does prison work?*, London 1997.

Szczepaniak P., *The prison sentence vs. education*, Kalisz – Warsaw 2003.

The act from 6th June 1997. Penal executive code, 'The Journal of Laws of the Republic of Poland' 1997, 5th of August.

www.sw.gov.pl/index.php/statystyki.

Zimring F. E., *The great american crime decline*, Oxford – New York 2007.

Teresa
Sołtysiak

Pathological behavior of young generation – several remarks on academic research and its relations with prevention and social rehabilitation

Introduction

For many centuries adults and now more and more often also young people have been entangled in pathological phenomena (Pospiszyl, 2008). And the development of civilization brings in new threats, such as: Internet addiction, tan-addiction, addiction to mobile phones or some other forms of already existing pathological phenomena, among others sponsoring of women by men, or men being sponsored by women as a manifestation of particular form of prostitution (Cyborska, 2005; Roberts, 2007; Kozak, 2007). Throughout the ages there were various reasons why people 'were dragged' under the influence of particular pathological phenomena, but the sociological and technical progresses even expanded the number of those reasons. As a result, there are many unidentified causative factors that lead to pathological behavior, for instance feeling of social inequality and of a worse position in the environment. Besides, pathological phenomena more and more often do not appear in isolated forms but in specific sets of links and relationships. It is important to say that those 'old' pathological phenomena appear now in a little altered form, whilst the 'new' ones may give some temporary subjective benefits to the people who are 'under their influence'. The more people are 'entangled' the bigger is their suffering, loss, pain and damage, including bio-psycho-social degradation. And their problems are not harmless or unimportant to their closer and distant social milieu.

This indication of problems related to phenomenal forms of social pathologies proves that they constitute a significant issue. The aforementioned facts confirm that there are nowadays more and more young people under the influence of pathologies, which even escalates the importance of the problem. After all, this young generation will in the near future direct and influence social and cultural development.

The paper herein is only a 'small share' in the process of analysis of pathological behavior of young generations. The author attempted to present several remarks on academic research concentrated on phenomenal forms of social pathologies among the young people with consideration for preventive and resocialization measures.

Selected directions of research concentrated on pathological behavior of young generation and their relation to practical activity

There are numerous theories, concepts and studies that may be helpful in explaining the reasons for people's behavior, and among them a significant position is taken by these which explain the factors and mechanisms of pathological behaviors. Generally speaking, the search for reasons for pathological behaviors has been looked onto from three perspectives:

- The first is a bio-psychological one – here, the causative factors of pathological behavior are searched for among somatic, physiological, neurophysiologic, intellectual, psychological determinants and many other features and personal predispositions of an individual, including his or her genetic qualities and innate characteristic.
- The second course is referred to as a socio-cultural one. Here, the reasons for pathological behavior are searched for in the conditions of social life, in both close and distant social milieu. In other words, they are searched in macro- and micro-social conditions in such areas as: political and economic conditions that to a certain extent delineate social and living standards of an individual. In relation to the aforementioned, cultural determinants are also taken into consideration and with them sub-cultural co-relations and all other influences and impacts of the environment, including a widely understood socialization of an individual and possibilities to meet one's own needs in the environment.
- The third perspective is called eclectic or mixed, or sometimes referred to as interdisciplinary or multifactorial; here the search for reasons for pathological behavior is concentrated on both bio-psychological and socio-cultural factors, with consideration for own activeness of an individual (Ciosek, 1996; Sołtysiak, 1995; Szczęsny, 2003).

In the works of scientists much attention is given to theories and concepts that explain the reasons for pathological behavior of young generation. It must be emphasized that many of these works constitute a wide compendium of knowledge from the fields of etiology, often combined with phenomenology and effects of pathological behavior.

The scientists have also tried and they still try to work out theories, concepts and studies that would allow explicating the causes, extent and intensity of particular pathological phenomena, the levels of empirical verification of which are various. Among the theories worth being mentioned there are:

General Theory of Genetic and Dynamic Crime Determinants by L. Lernell; Theory of Diversified Connections by E. H. Sutherland; Control Theory by W. C. Reckless; Theory of Hirschi;

Power-Control Theory of J. Hagan, A. R. Gillis, J. Simpson and others (Lernell, 1973; Siemaszko, 1993; Sołtysiak, 2003).

It must be mentioned, however, that in each of the above methods of research and in verifications of theories, the study concentrated on the search for factors that cause pathological behavior of young generations is carried out with consideration for and application of varied methodological assumptions. That results mainly from the fact that the study is carried out by scientists with different knowledge of the subject: teachers, sociologists, psychologists, criminologists and others, who assume and accept methodology, characteristic for and applied in a particular field of science. It does not mean that these solutions are wrong, on the contrary – the research conducted by scientists specializing in various areas widens and deepens our knowledge of the subject.

Considering the size of this paper, it would be impossible to present all methodological solutions with all their good and bad sides. Besides, the author does not feel competent to do that. However, it seems justified to refer to methodological assumptions of studies of socialization, as the paper discusses the issues concerning young generation. Moreover, in favor of such solution argues the fact that this society, unfortunately, generates pathological behavior. Besides, in the process of a widely understood socialization positive and negative influences and relations intertwine and it is difficult to determine such environment where a young person could be under the influence of unambiguously positive or negative stimuli coming from the environment (Kowalski, 1994).

Therefore, in broad outline, methodological assumptions connected with the study of socialization of young generation take into consideration the following scientific approaches:

Methodological approach of positivist direction (Tillmann, 1993). With this approach, the study is based on highly standardized set of research instruments. A pilot study that usually precedes the real study allows to modify and improve research instruments.

Within the scope of such study there is young generation - a group of several dozen or sometimes a few hundred people, selected with consideration for some particular criteria chosen by a researcher or researchers. Thus, a 'random sample' is selected with respect to specific socio-demographic or biographic features. The results obtained from such study allow to carry out various analyses - quantitative and often based on statistical methods. Such results are most frequently generalized to a wider community of young people. Thus, they give the possibility to determine the causes, dimensions and even the effects of analyzed pathological behavior of young generations. Moreover, they may constitute guidelines on preventive and social rehabilitation measures that need to be taken.

This scientific approach has both good and bad sides. Its positive aspects are, among others: carefully prepared set of research instruments, often preceded by several pilot studies, accurate selection of a generation to be analyzed, wide possibilities to process gathered empirical data with application of numerous statistical methods that deepen the quantitative analyses. And this all gives a possibility to obtain and reveal a wider spectrum of the analyzed issues. Moreover, the results of analyses allow to make comparisons, generalization, observations and conclusions concerning a larger population of young people. In other words, such type of research shows a certain picture of pathological phenomenon or phenomena of the youth.

However, there are also negative aspects of such study, for instance: selection of a representative sample with consideration for particular features, e.g. complete and incomplete family structure, which may affect and mark young generation. However, even if this difficulty is overcome by the researcher with no stigmatization of young people, the others shall emerge. A group of young people involved in the study, although selected according to some particular criteria, when responding to questions may not reveal the actual information concerning their lives and their 'participation' in the analyzed pathological phenomenon or phenomena. They may also choose random answers. As a consequence, the results obtained shall be distorted, and gathered empirical data shall lead to wrong conclusions and generalizations. What is more, apart from filtering questions, there are few possibilities to contrast and confirm obtained empirical data. Therefore, the researcher may only believe in honesty of responders and assume their truthfulness. Besides, such study hinders a deeper and more insightful recognition of the occurrence of particular pathological phenomenon among the young and others.

It is obvious that there are many positive and negative aspects of such study. The author has no intentions of criticizing it, however. She would rather present possible good and bad sides of this research.

Another methodological approach applied in the study of socialization and its disturbances among young people is the one oriented towards hermeneutics and understanding. Here the research covers 'small random samples', i.e. the groups consisting of between a few and several people. In such study the researcher attempts to explore the nature of causes and effects, and also of consequences of pathological behavior of the analyzed group. For this study mutually complementing and supplementing sets of research instruments are used. Such approach allows to observe various connections and co-relations between apparently unimportant or insignificant events from young people's lives, which may determine their choices in life, very often inconsistent with what the society expects from them.

This study is carried out individually, frequently within the environment where an individual exists, which makes it even more credible, especially that it is substantiated by observations. The results must not be generalized or related to a wider group of young people.

Quite insightful analysis of young generation concerned constitutes a positive aspect of such study. This study allows to observe different areas of life and, what is even more important, to find the causative factors that might provoke pathological behavior, to observe forms and types of such behavior, its intensity and subjective effects.

There are however some negative aspects of the study, such as: long periods of research which may discourage young people or even make them withdraw from the study. Moreover, the research may evoke young people's unpleasant memories and thus worsen their problems with adaptation, which they may try to neutralize with other pathological activities. The results of this study must not be generalized, and the conclusions made must not be related to other members of the youth. So, they can be only or as much as useful in designing preventive or social rehabilitation actions for young people that take part in the study.

The above mentioned approaches have their supporters and opponents. In fact, both their positive and negative sides should be taken into consideration, as such awareness allows to improve quality of the study. Quite often both of the aforementioned areas of studies are combined, i.e. qualitative and quantitative. Thanks to such strategy a wider group of young people can be involved in the study, which means it is more representative and allows a better recognition of phenomenal forms of pathologies occurring among young persons. Besides, such combined form of study takes into consideration mutual relations and connections between pathological phenomena, their impact on lives and existence of respondents.

Apart from that, the analyses of phenomenal forms of social pathologies of young people involve, though quite rarely, catamnestic studies. This type of study is characterized by a long-lasting observation of lives of the people included in the research. Such studies allow gaining a deep knowledge of causes but also of intensity or regression of particular examined pathological phenomenon or phenomena among the analyzed subjects (Żabczyńska, 1981; Urban, Stanik, 2008). However, such study causes many difficulties, for instance related to the fact that the respondents change their place of residence, which in turn prevents further research. Besides, the studies are most frequently carried out by a researcher with the aim to obtain academic degree, and long-lasting catamnestic studies rather do not help in such case.

There is no doubt, however, that any studies that allow to recognize, discover and present the causes, dimension and also the effects of pathological behavior are of a great significance. No matter what methodological solutions and scientific orientation or direction have been assumed by a researcher, the study reveals a picture of distorted reality in which some of young people exist. We must admit that many studies are being carried out, but the reality is not constant and is a subject to continuous changes. That is why it is crucial to carry out further research covering wider and wider spectrum of factors that provoke pathological behavior of young people as well as of phenomenology of such behavior.

Here, however, other difficulties related to analyses of young people arise. First of all, a researcher must obtain various permits, including permissions of the respondents themselves. And young people are not always 'willing' to participate in such studies, as quite frequently they are afraid that their 'hidden' negative actions may be 'brought to light'. As a result, as it has been indicated herein, they give inadequate answers, and hinder the researcher's work. Besides, if young people are not yet 18 years old, the consent of parents (guardians) must be obtained for participation in the study. But parents (or guardians) are also not very eager to allow their children participate in such undertaking, or sometimes they give their consent but under certain conditions, for instance: questions that may reveal the true state of family life should be omitted. Considering the fact that one's own family constitutes the core of socialization activities, approval of such condition is impossible. There are also other situations – parents give their consent, research is carried out and completed, the data are gathered and then parents protest, which makes the researchers start their work again from the very beginning. Moreover, if the study is carried out in educational institution or schools, persons employed there may also disagree on the research.

However, if the above and some other difficulties (there may be many more) have been finally overcome by the researchers, many of which manage to do so and here we must take our hats off, another thought emerges. When should the studies concerning phenomenal forms of pathologies among young people be carried out? Although the answer seems to be quite simple – that there should be catamnestic studies carried out with the largest samples possible and in the earliest possible period of life, in order to take the necessary and proper preventive and resocialization measures based on the gathered data. On the other hand, such early studies may cause negative effects. After all, they may provoke very young people to negative actions. Another question is how to select the persons at risk and provide them with proper preventive and resocialization actions, if the studies are usually anonymous, since the respondents as a rule do not give their consent to another type of studies.

However, if the studies are carried out late, when an individual is already deeply entangled in pathological behavior, which means that a serious degradation of features and predispositions of just developing personality of a growing up individual took place, the picture and results are distorted. The results of such study, despite the proper choice of research instruments and despite the accuracy of analysis, are not really credible. Saying succinctly – either 'the time has deformed' the factual picture of reasons, or the occurring personality disorder does not allow to reveal a real nature of the problem.

Thus, it is quite difficult to combine gathered results with practical activity. Besides, one must not forget about the binding regulations which are not always optimal. The Juvenile Justice Act of 1982 may be mentioned here as an example of such regulations. This Act has been widely discussed and many times criticized. Some amendments to the Act were introduced in the 1990s, but it is difficult to say, whether the solutions taken have been proper. Several problems seems still unsolved, such as the issue of social rehabilitation in open environment, among others parental authority limitation and entrusting grandparents with the sole responsibility for young generation in the situation when all three generations reside in one place.

Another problem constitutes social rehabilitation of juvenile in penitentiary. Individualization of such process can only be dreamt of. The reality is such: one educationist or pedagogue looks after even 100 inmates.

Considering centers for addictions – they are usually overcrowded. Even if a young person 'gets to' such centre, his or her social rehabilitation period is usually reduced, often due to lack of space and 'economic calculation of the centre', which is unfortunately not a beneficial solution.

In this paper only some improprieties concerning legal regulations, affecting preventive and social rehabilitation measures, have been mentioned. However, all the facts give an impression that the studies are carried out separately from the practical activities with no co-relation between them, and that preventive and social rehabilitation actions run their own, different course. Maybe it would be reasonable to apply the results of research in practical activities on a wider scale. Maybe in certain regions the research centers and the institutions that deal with practical actions should tighten their cooperation. Then, the results of research could have been used not only for scientific development, which is obviously extremely important, but they would also help with bringing young people back to the society – and these actions are the most vital! There is only one problem – how to do it, when the studies are anonymous and data protection is binding? So, even the potential cooperation and early discovery of disorders will not be enough if certain, optimal legal regulations are not introduced.

Conclusion

This paper comprises several remarks on connections and relations between scientific studies and preventive and social rehabilitation activities.

Despite various obstacles, it is obvious that only studies carried out in diversified areas by different specialists may result in a wide recognition of the causes, symptoms, dimension and consequences of pathological behavior of young people. No matter if the studies are qualitative, quantitative or qualitative-quantitative; they are all good and proper, on the condition that they are carried out diligently and appropriately. It is important, however, that the results of studies were more often applied in practice. It is how the optimal solutions should be searched for: by adapting legal regulations and through cooperation of research centers and institutions dealing with preventive and social rehabilitation activities, including social rehabilitation of young generation.

References

Ciosek M., *Człowiek w obliczu izolacji więziennej*, Gdańsk 1996.

Cyborska M., *Student/ka po godzinach*, „Semestr" 2005, 3.

Guerreschi C., *Nowe uzależnienia*, Kraków 2005.

Hołyst B., *Kryminologia*, Warszawa 1994.

Kowalski S., *Socjologia wychowania*, Warszawa 2004.

Kozak S., *Patologie wśród dzieci i młodzieży*, Warszawa 2007.

Lernell L., *Zarys kryminologii ogólnej*, przeł. A. Wieczorek-Niebielska, Warszawa 1973.

Pospiszyl I., *Patologie społeczne*, Warszawa 2008.

Roberts N., *Dziwki w historii. Prostytucja w społeczeństwie zachodnim*, przeł. L. Engelking, Warszawa 2007.

Siemaszko A., *Granice tolerancji, o teoriach zachowań dewiacyjnych*, Warszawa 1993.

Sołtysiak T., *Socjalizacja a zaburzenia w zachowaniach młodzieży* [w:] T. Sołtysiak (red.), *Zagrożenia w wychowaniu i socjalizacji młodzieży oraz możliwości ich przezwyciężania*, Bydgoszcz 2003.

Sołtysiak T., *Uwarunkowania środowiskowe i determinanty subiektywne uczestnictwa nieletnich w podkulturach*, Bydgoszcz 1995.

Szczęsny W., *Zarys resocjalizacji z elementami patologii społecznej i profilaktyki*, Warszawa 2003.

Tillmann K. J., *Teorie socjalizacji. Społeczność, instytucja, upodmiotowienie*, przeł. G. Bluszcz, B. Miracki, Warszawa 1993.

Urban B., Stanik J. M. (red.), *Resocjalizacja*, t. 1, Warszawa 2008.

Żabczyńska E., *Przestępczość dzieci*, Warszawa 1981.

Ewa Murawska

The identity of an elderly person in the postmodern world – crisis or a new quality?

Introduction

One of the problems concerning the most crucial educational dilemmas which reflect radical changes in living conditions, social relations and the anticipation of what the future may bring is the question: how, in modern reality, is the identity of a man constituted if his/her adolescence and youth fell on the 'previous period'? Does an elderly person experience any identity crisis, and if so, for what reasons? Inspiration for searching the answers to such posed questions may be the propositions of Z. Bauman, in whose opinion a man convinced that the world is organised according to some order aspired to a complete and consistent construction of identity. Today those identifying points (points of reference), or laws considered universal have lost their stability or validity, that is why post-modernity means

> [...] a lack of clearly defined identity; the less precisely defined identity is, the better for its holder [...] Strictly post-modern personality is distinguished by a lack of identity (Bauman, 1994, p. 16).

However, life outside identity, without any sense of belonging, arouses fear. A way out from that situation, as T. Szkudlarek suggests, is to accustom oneself to ambivalence, to domesticate it (1995, p. 250). Certainly, it brings a question: does such freely constructed identity enlarge the sphere of man's freedom and, what is more important in such situation, the multiplicity or certainty of choice? Does a vague (unstable) identity give a chance for sovereign choices? These questions gain particular importance when it is so difficult for a modern man to build his/her own identifications in the time of crisis, degeneration, vagueness, dispersal, undermining the validity of so far prevailing moral and axiological codes, deterioration of the prestige of intellectual elites, the fall of authorities and, simultaneously, in the world of global challenges, reckless consumerism, broad access to mass culture and information (reaching the state of information noise or gibberish). According to Z. Kwieciński, those phenomena pose a threat of social anomie, and lead to destabilising the sense of identity, to pathological forms of blocking or prolonging the identity crisis (1990, p. 333). It is little convincing, however, that facing difficulties in self-defining, the modern man consciously renounces building his own identity, defining himself in the world of 'ambiguity of meanings' and radical change, which raises helplessness among elderly people more than in other groups. Searching the answer to the question: who am I, contrary to expectations, gains particular significance today, also in the context of (not)dealing with loss, estrangement, frustration in the world void of stable and trustworthy sign-posts. As Ch. Taylor put it, identity is that without which 'we don't know who we are, what our culture is, what heroes we should imitate and what daemons avoid, where we come from and what our destination is' (cited after: Misztal, 2005, p. 26). The dramatic position of a man of the 21 century Z. Bauman describes as follows:

> Life in the society of fluid modernity cannot stay in one place. It has to update itself (that is everyday to get rid of features and attributes that are not valid anymore, as well as to add/reject identities created/put together at the moment) – otherwise it will pine away. Life in the society of fluid modernity, hurried by a specter of expiry, goes on fast. [...] Now we need to run for our life to stay at the spot, away from the garbage bin where all the marauders end up (Bauman, 2007, p. 8).

What with those who cannot keep up, with those who walk at a slower pace?

(Un)fulfillment phase in a cycle of life

Human life is divided by psychology and sociology into different cycles and phases, perceived as stages, with developmental tasks typical for those stages. The life-span concepts of developmental psychology assume that a person develops through all his/her life, with different tasks to complete during that time, solving problems which pose challenges and stimulate internal development[1]. Development means reaching the optimal level of dealing with problems, self-fulfillment, finding the joy of life and meaning of professional and social activity. On the efficacy of completing the incoming tasks and coping with crises depends the quality, sense of fulfillment and meaning of a human life, successful accomplishment of next developmental stages, and willingness to undertake tasks in next phases of life.

---

[1] In the *life-span* approach development may take place in all periods of life, while traditional approach attributes development to the childhood and adolescence period, stability to adulthood, and developmental regress to old age.

Theories emphasising the meaning of activity and experience in anticipating developmental changes include the theory of seasons of life by D. Levinson (cf Trempała, 2000, p. 267 and after). Periodicity and changeability of human life are described here by references to metaphors of seasons, travel; explaining phenomena typical of development in adulthood through analogy with wandering, proceeding, or the effort of cognition.

The term 'cycle of life'[2] is attributed by scientist to multiple restructuring of life from childhood to adulthood, where the path of life consists of a periodically recurring building, usage and modifying of life structures[3]. Early adulthood (17–45 years) is, according to D. Levinson, the peak of physical strength, the time of investing in future, building intellectual prowess, the time of professional and personal independence. Mid-life era (40-60 years) is the time of stabilisation of the life structure, 'reaping the fruits', reaching consistency between life experience and individual I, integration of plans and desires, a period of fulfillment in different fields of life (cf Brzezińska, Appelt, Wojciechowska, 2002, pp. 12–15). While late adulthood (after 60) is the time of changes in social relations, ending professional activity, focus on biopsychosocial needs related to age. This period requires accepting transition, achieving internal harmony, using one's own internal resources, experience and life wisdom, which is conducive of taking up the role of a counselor, a mentor, a person ready to provide support. The sequences of life periods listed above have the same value for the development whose climax is the stabilising of the life structure (cf Trempała, 2000, p. 268).

The so-called mixed, multi-dimensional models of development include the concept by M. Tyszkowa, who treats adulthood as the basic phase of human life. Objectively, adulthood is defined by chronological frames, whereas subjectively – by impressions of a man who, on the basis of life experiences, finds himself an independent and mature person. Therefore, adulthood does not occur at the same time for all people, and it last until a very old age constituting an integral part of adulthood. Developmental process, according to Tyszkowa, is a process of constant changes resulting from the participation of an individual in different life situations, from organisation of the structures of individual experience and from their modification. In the process of developmental changes a crucial significance is attributed here to the individual's activity towards change, his/her relation to

---

[2] D. Levinson distinguished four main 25-year-long eras in the life cycle, divided into developmental periods according to biopsychological differences. Those are: pre-adulthood era (0–22 years); early adulthood era (17–45 years); mid-adulthood era (40–65 years); late adulthood (60 years and more).

[3] Life structure according to D. Levinson is, basic at different life stages, a model of a person's activity and his/her relations with the surroundings: culture, institutions, social groups and individuals.

the environment and to experience related to satisfaction of needs (cf Tyszkowa, 1988, p. 12).

According to E. H. Erikson's concept, the old age in the life cycle (phase VIII) denotes vitality and attempts to balance the tensions between life integrity (the sense of consistency and completeness) and stimulae leading to despair, hopelessness and a sense of failure (cf Witkowski, 2000, pp. 147–153). What takes place here is

> the greatest existential tension between potentials of development.[...] in the positive sense it is possible to achieve completion of all the previous, necessary steps in development, while in the negative sense, it is defined by a threat of complete existential degradation, throwing an individual's functional potential from the highest point at the developmental ladder to the point of departure (*ibidem*, p. 148).

Especially noteworthy is the threat to a person's identity and three types of identity confusion, which impair his/her development: developmental identity crisis, identity confusion and identity takeover (cf *ibidem*, pp. 119–153). Senior age is the time of achieving wisdom, integration of ego, making a balance of one's life, which leads to acceptance of the situation or to a sense of regret. It is the time of making a balance of successes and failures, accepting the life lived so far (at the same time, accepting death), or a sense of failure, causing despair and hopelesness. Thus, it could be said that identity confusion in an elderly person is analogical to that of an adolescent, however, the peculiarity of the situation of elderly people lies in the fact that this is a generation whose habits (defining identity) were formed in the previous, non-existent system, and 'breaking free from the past is not easy' (Bugajska, 2006, p. 133). Even less so since, as B. Synak notices (after: *ibidem*), there is a stir in the collective memory of the oldest generation, and the social depreciation of the previous period undermines the basis of their identity. Moreover, the odium of ideologically discredited generation attributed to them, with the stigma of 'sins' of the old times not only impedes creation of a complete identity, but increases the distance between generations and deepens the old age crisis. 'An elderly person in the modern world seems to defend his/her identity balancing between passive adjustment and dependence on the one hand, and active participation and autonomy on the other' (*ibidem*, p. 138). E. Erikson completing the concept of psychosocial identity stipulated that identity is 'a style of synthesising experience' (cited after: Witkowski, 2007, p. 217).

> The analysis of the style in which an individual [...] deals with conflicting content of that experience allows for – says L. Witkowski – describing e.g. the level of competence in dealing with existential tasks in the cycle of life (*ibidem*).

Increasingly inadequate learned collective identity of elderly people necessitates searching for new models and rules of behaviour. 'The existing identity crisis may lead to withdrawal, conformism, rebellion, innovative behaviour, transfer of loyalty' (Bugajska, 2006, p. 136). Two extreme poles in the behaviour of elderly people can be distinguished: from hiding in a peculiar social niche, which designates lack of acceptance for changes, for what modernity is defining, from defiance towards changes, submitting to marginalization in social life to impressive activity for one's environment, satisfactory engagement in family affairs and other matters, working for non-government organisations, self-help groups, associations, various forms of adult education etc., that is a fulfillment creativity.

The problems of the identity of an elderly person

Longevity, and even immortality, are among man's permanent dreams. Although along with the development of civilisation the average life expectancy is increasing, the quality of life of senior citizens[4], conditioned by many subjective and objective factors, is deteriorating. Getting older, understood literally, means changes that a person undergoes with the passing of time, so it actually lasts throughout whole life. Surely it may be seen as a gradual process of loss (of skills, health, beauty, social status etc.), but it may also mean a life-long process of enriching physical, psychological, cultural, economic, spiritual and other aspects of our existence. According to a recent doctrine of ageism, the reason for deteriorating quality of lives of elderly people is their discrimination on the basis of old age[5]. Senior discrimination factors include doubtlessly enforced retiring[6], conditioning medical treatment and insurance on a patient's age, and the critical point of retiring itself, which designates 'social senility'. Nowadays the last factor gains particular status in the view of challenges the modern man is facing, which often leads to his loss, helplessness and a 'threatened identity' syndrome. In case of important social changes, frustrations which may be referred to as identity frustrations concern whole social groups and societies. However, faced with disappearance of thus far existing and recognised ways of 'domesticating

---

[4] Senior is a common term denoting a person with the longest life or working experience in a clan, family, team, society. Cf. *Słownik języka polskiego PWN*, 1989, p. 196; E. H. Erikson believes the senior age to be the time of achieving wisdom, integration of ego, when making a balance of one's life leads to acceptance or regret, in: Witkowski, 2000; the starting point of old age is conventionally the age at which a person gains a legal right to retire, that is 60 years for women and 65 for men.

[5] Different cultures allocate different positions to old people – some value them for their wisdom and experience, bestowing social prestige and authority on them; other push them into the margin of solitude, treating them as useless burden.

[6] Retiring mechanism of isolation and social segregation may be treated as a kind of violence, since by treating all people equally, it limits individuality and autonomy of an individual (this is so-called isonomie trap, that is limiting the rights of elderly people); after: Bugajska, 2006, 2(15), p. 134.

in the world', it is an elderly person who finds the task of finding a place in a new, radically changing reality particularly difficult, as s/he is obliged to search for a way to become enrooted, or experience 'social exile' (cf. Bugajska, 2006, p. 133). At the same time modernity promotes strong, young, successful people, determined to create their spectacular careers. It seems that these times are not favourable for elderly people, particularly experiencing social marginalisation, or even exclusion. Variety and richness of the modern world's offers (even the excess of offers) necessitates making often difficult choices, also of a life path and a lifestyle, that is defining one's identity in completely new social and cultural conditions. As H. Kwiatkowska writes, today

> [...] the past loses its meaning. The world's changeability causes fathers' wisdom being discredited by their children. Thus the conclusion that past ages have less and less to say in what the world is and could be, how a man should be prepared to live in that world (Kwiatkowska, 1997, pp. 13–14).

Conclusion

The prospect of staying active in old age may have a positive impact on personal choices taken in earlier stages of life, and preparing whole populations to late stages in life should doubtlessly become an integral part of a country's social policy. It is also, I emphasise, a task for pedagogues[7]. The pedagogical context of the problem mentioned concentrates around the question: can one prepare for old age and what are the conditions of successful ageing? Longitudinal research carried out since 1940s confirms that the best prognosis for the late period of life is a successful stage between the 30. and 50. year of a person's life. A happy childhood in a caring, warm environment is likewise important for successful ageing, and also such factors as: self esteem, flexibility, personal control over one's life, adaptation to a role (I refer to: Halicki, Halicka, 2005, p. 139). Preparing for old age, seen from the perspective of a teacher, means supporting the development of interests, forming healthy lifestyle habits, healthy diet, proper spending of free time, that is forming proper habits and skills. It also means creating such pedagogical situations as favour building one's self esteem, courage in undertaking ambitious plans, and conscious shaping of a fulfilled, satisfactory future, also a distant one, almost abstract from the perspective of a young person. Since, referring to Z. Bauman's reflection on life in the world of uncertainty:

---

[7] Social arguments (equal treatment for problems of all social groups), demographic arguments (statistics point to a growing tendency for the Polish society to get older), as well as economic arguments ('happy old age' is cheaper) support this view.

Life in a society of fluid modernity is a gloomy, for played seriously, version of the musical chairs game. At the real stakes of the race is the (temporary) safety from joining the ranks of those excluded, and staying away from a garbage bin (2007, pp. 8–9).

Under the conditions of thus far unknown speed of changes, 'identity frustrations' concern first and foremost, which I emphasize, the representatives of the oldest generation, belonging to two different social 'worlds', the participants and witnesses of transition from 'modernity' to 'post-modernity'[8]. Today it seems mandatory to think in terms of the future, anticipating changes in the context of global processes. The past loses its significance, although it rings in often traumatic experiences of people whose childhood and youth fell on the times in all aspects far from modernity. It is thus a generation doomed to confront the matter not only unknown, but in itself unpredictable, new, carrying a potential of many opportunities and chances, but also fears and threats.

For never before – according to Z. Cackowski – has a man forming his life been so devoid of strength derived form the journey endured, never before, to such extent, has he been left to himself in creating his reality (Kwiatkowska, 1997, p. 14).

Ageing means not only biological changes that a man experiences with time, but it is a lifelong process of enriching the psychological, cultural and spiritual aspects of our existence.

References

Bauman Z., *Płynne życie*, Kraków 2007.

Bauman Z., *Ponowoczesne wzory osobowe* [w:] Z. Bauman, *Dwa szkice o moralności ponowoczesnej*, Warszawa 1994.

Brzezińska A., Appelt K., Wojciechowska J. (red.), *Szanse i zagrożenia dla rozwoju w okresie dorosłości*, Poznań 2002.

Bugajska B., *Człowiek stary wobec zagrożeń współczesności*, „Edukacja Humanistyczna" 2006, 2(15).

Halicki J., Halicka M., *Rola nauczyciela w przygotowaniu do starości* [w:] W. Horner, M. S. Szymański (red.), *Nauczyciel i kształcenie nauczycieli. Zmiany i wyzwania*, Warszawa 2005.

Kwiatkowska H., *Edukacja nauczycieli. Konteksty – kategorie – praktyki*, Warszawa 1997.

---

[8] Aptly put by the author of the article referred to: *An elderly person and the threats of modernity.*

Kwieciński Z., *Sytuacja anomii społecznej jako blokada rozwoju młodzieży ku orientacji etycznej* [w:] Z. Kwieciński, L. Witkowski (red.), *Ku pedagogii pogranicza*, Toruń 1990.

Miluska J., *Tożsamość kobiet i mężczyzn w cyklu życia*, Poznań 1996.

Misztal B., *Tożsamość jako pojęcie i zjawisko społeczne w zderzeniu z procesami globalizacji* [w:] E. Budakowska (red.), *Tożsamość bez granic. Współczesne wyzwania*, Warszawa 2005.

Słownik języka polskiego PWN, Warszawa 1989.

Szkudlarek T., *Szkic nienowoczesny o okolicach wychowania* [w:] A. Seidler-Janiszewska (red.), *Trudna ponowoczesność. Rozmowy z Zygmuntem Baumanem*, Poznań 1995.

Trempała J., *Koncepcje rozwoju człowieka* [w:] J. Strelau (red.), *Psychologia, podręcznik akademicki*, t. 1, Gdańsk 2000.

Turner J. S., Helms D. B., *Rozwój człowieka*, przeł. S. Lis, Warszawa 1999.

Tyszkowa M. (red.), *Rozwój psychiczny w ciągu życia. Zagadnienia teoretyczne i metodologiczne*, Warszawa 1988.

Witkowski L., *Edukacja wobec sporów o (po)nowoczesność*, t. 1, Warszawa 2007.

Witkowski L., *Rozwój i tożsamość w cyklu życia. Studium koncepcji Erika H. Eriksona*, Toruń 2000.

Danuta
Apanel

Mentally handicapped people and their leisure time

'Leisure time' as a definition appeared and got in use in June 1957 when it was approved by The International Conference of UNECSO. At the beginning the concept of leisure time was replaced by such word as holiday or recreation, but as its idea comprised many social situations, it was specified due to the main differences in spending leisure time by children, young people and adults (Ploch, 1992, p. 4).

The concept leisure time of children, young people and adults by most authors is defined as

> [...] a social value that has been earned by an individual (society) for their personal development and relaxation. [...]; the leisure time of children, young people and adults is the time that they can organize on their own, in the ways they want to, according to their needs and interests, no matter what forms have they chosen (*ibidem*, p. 5).

The leisure time spent by mentally handicapped people can be described as

> this period of a day that is left after learning at a special education institution or at work, after basic body regeneration, medical treatment and completion of daily chores. The time is managed and organized by themselves for their relaxation, entertainment and developing personal interests (*ibidem*).

The mentally handicapped have special requirements for their development and because of that, their leisure time should be organized, just to satisfy their needs.

The appropriate organizing of their leisure time plays an important role in their bio psychical lives, keeping balance of the central nervous system that is indispensable for their proper functioning. That is why a special attention should be paid to create good proportions in organizing their free time in the way that allows them to ease tension and keep them in a good mood.

There are a few perspectives when we think about leisure time and the mentally handicapped, especially if it is to be treated not only as a social issue but also a great educational value.

We can name such aspects as: an educational aspect, a psychological aspect, a tutelary aspect, a curative aspect and a rehabilitation aspect.

Educational and psychological aspect

The general trait of mentally handicapped children and young people is the low level of orientation in perceiving reality. Their psychological life is poor and the disturbances of their cognitive processes result in disturbances of the other processes.

Their leisure time may be the source of many additional experiences and may cause vivid psychophysical responses. The feelings of great satisfaction, joy and happiness are typical for them. The activities involving intellectual efforts such as learning at school or working may not result in relaxation or releasing their mental tension.

The possibility of spending the leisure time actively, in an organized way can stimulate them, shape and enrich their personalities as well as shows their attitudes, dreams, ideals and views. For the mentally handicapped their leisure time is an opportunity to act spontaneously and develop their interests (Ploch, 1992, pp. 9–12).

Tutelary aspect

The basic conception of tutelar pedagogy is supporting the development of the mentally handicapped, creating favourable conditions for their existence and shaping their personalities in a complex way.

The proper organizing of their leisure time contributes to their positive emotional mood and the favourable atmosphere of their life environment.

The main aims are to create the family atmosphere and to help with problem solving. The main directions of organizing the leisure time for the mentally handicapped are:
a) health and safety,
b) compensative activities,
c) preventing difficulties and failures,
d) improving life environment,
e) providing all possible benefits (*ibidem*, pp. 12–13).

Curative aspect

Leisure time has also a curative aspect as it has a significant impact on a psychophysical relaxation of the organism that is released from the intellectual effort and, very often, from the unfavourable conditions of an educational institution.

Fresh, healthy air and physical activity are important factors for developing muscle and bone systems and general physical and motoric condition.

Plays, games, rehabilitation exercises provide many positive emotions, toughen up body, develop skills and regulate metabolism (*ibidem*, pp. 13–14).

Rehabilitation aspect

Rehabilitation means to bring back to health those who have been deprived one or more functions of their body.

In more general concept it can be described as a set of comprehensive, educational activities, tailored to the needs and abilities of the mentally handicapped to support their complete psychophysical development.

The main characteristic of these activities is

the widest possible development of the least affected functions by strengthening and improving their mental and physical abilities and replacing biological and developmental deficiencies (*ibidem*, p. 15).

The modern forms of organizing leisure time appeared in the second half of the previous century. Their simplest classification goes in a following way:

Table 1. Modern ways of spending leisure time

Ways of spending leisure time	
1.	Tourism
2.	Sport
3.	Mass media
4.	Theatres, concerts, exhibitions and museums
5.	Self-education
6.	Amateur activities
7.	Do-it-yourself activities
8.	Amateur animal breeding
9.	Group activities, games and plays
10.	Collecting
11.	Social activities

Source: Pięta, 2004.

The most popular and the most time-consuming forms of spending leisure time are tourism, sport and mass media. They are practised by the greatest number of people.

Tourism is the most expansive kind of modern holidays as well as the most popular and practised by millions of Poles.

> Tourism is an activity practised outside the place of permanent residence, connected to cognitive aims and some sport elements (Pięta, 2004, p. 82).

It comprises any forms of changing a place of residence not connected to a job or a change in place of living.

Tourism has many functions such as: a curative, relaxing, cultural, cognitive, educational and economic. It is usually treated as a form of physical activity or sightseeing.

T. Łobożewicz and G. Bieńczyk (2001) in their work name nine types of tourism: mass tourism, alternative tourism, active tourism, qualified tourism, business tourism, ethnic tourism, social tourism pilgrimages, sightseeing and some other forms connected to each of these types.

Nowadays sport is practised by many people and is also a kind of a great event that is able to attract a great number of spectators raising their emotions. Sport is also an important factor for integrating different social groups not only in a local environment but also on the regional and international scale.

> Sport is a conscious and voluntary activity that is performed by humans to satisfy their needs for playing, competitiveness and perfecting their own physical and mental features. Sport comprises exercises, games and play that are practised according to the specific rules (*ibidem*, p. 88).

However, two types of sports should be mentioned when we consider spending leisure time, namely sport as a spectacular event and practising sport.

In these two cases sport plays a great role in managing free time by great number of people.

Table 2. Sport classification

Type of sport		Characteristics
Qualified	Practising	Professional sport is not a part of leisure time. No matter what a formal status of a competitor is, trainings and competitions are his job.
	Interest	For millions of people in the world sport events play an important role in managing their leisure time.
Recreation sport		Recreation sport is practised by amateurs in their leisure time. It is an authentic free time activity. It can be practised individually or in teams.

Disabled sports	Disabled sport is a form of physical activity that improves physical condition of the disabled and is an important element of their rehabilitation.

Source: Pięta, 2004.

Another form are mass media. These are facilities and institutions whose task is to direct some contents to numerous and differentiated audiences: the press, radio, televison, phonography (records, cassettes), films widely distributed by cinemas, video, dvd and books published in extended editions. Their main characteristic is the wide range of their audience.

They help to satisfy the needs connected to all functions of leisure time, namely relaxation, entertainment and self-development.

Other classification of leisure time should be applied when considering the mentally handicapped. L. Ploch lists the following activities:

entertainment activities, tourism and sightseeing, sport activities, indor activities, DIY activities, hobby and arts, activities in local environment, participating in children and youth organizations, holidays and rehabilitation groups, organized holidays, mass media, institutions of culture, social life (Ploch, 1992, pp. 75–76).

Interesting forms of spending leisure time in all institutions are entertainment activities. They allow the mentally handicapped to spend their time in an attractive way, without involving considerable expenses or elaborated equipment.

These activities comprise: drama groups, art groups, dance groups, singing and music groups, table games, cultural events, TV and radio programmes and many others, including mass events. Such activities provide many emotions and experiences, contact with culture as well as help spark interests and hobbies.

Another form worth popularizing is tourism and sightseeing offering wide rehabilitation, educational and therapeutic values. As a form of spending free time, these activities provide

mental relaxation, satisfy the needs for physical activeness, raise the participants' optimism and belief in their abilities.

The mentally handicapped are very keen on sport, plays and games. These activities have significant social, relaxation and protective meanings.

Physical activity and special situations arising during games and plays have a therapeutic effects on the mental condition of the mentally handicapped, satisfy their physical activity needs, develop their motor abilities and character features such as: consistence, determination, co-operativeness and general ability of team work and competitiveness (*ibidem*, p. 78).

Not all forms of sport can be applied for the mentally handicapped but suitable activities, prepared by professional trainers and instructors, can improve their mental condition, raise optimism and eagerness to overcome difficulties, promote initiative and interests in physical exercises. The mentally handicapped children and young are more interested in active participation in games and plays, tournaments and competitions than in professional sports.

Indoor games and plays are also active forms of spending leisure time.

These types of activities favour entertainment and widely perceived engagement in cultural events. They not only bring the participants feeling of safety and help overcome difficulties but are also very popular because of their intimate and voluntary character, independence in organizing and arranging various activities that are matched according to the needs and abilities of all.

Other attractive forms are connected to do-it- yourself activities as they involve individual preferences and skills. Each participant can experience personal satisfaction from doing time-consuming tasks that stimulate his imagination and manual skills. Moreover, they learn how to operate tools and household devices, how to obey the rules of safety – the skills important for their independent existence and sense of self-esteem.

These forms can be organized in home-centred groups, do-it-yourself groups, modelling (aeromodelling, ship modelling), construction groups and many others.

Artistic and hobby groups may be part of this repertoire and they may have a significant impact on their participants' emotions.

Thus, chosen pursuits can be even wider than those offered by groups of interests or institutions. It is worth noticing that the charges tend to adapt such activities that provide exceptionally positive emotions. If their tutors/ therapists can involve them in appropriately chosen tasks, the participants will put a lot of physical and mental effort into

their work getting a lot of enjoyment and satisfaction.

Many institutions representing tourism, sport, theatre, arts, modelling, photography and so forth, may contribute to organizing a variety of events.

One of the most important forms is activiteness in the nearest environment. Children and young people get their experiences from different life situations. They are stimulated to take part in education and self-education processes in a natural way.

This form weighs in favour of its rehabilitation, therapeutic and educational values as it comprises useful activities for their groups, institutions, families, artistic, protective or service events, contacts with their environment.

The main idea behind the planning of leisure time is the active participation in various children and young people organisations.

> Their activities should not only match conditions in which the leisure time is organized, the needs of institutions and environment but also take into consideration the needs and abilities of individuals (Ploch, 1992, p. 82).

When we talk about the organisations, we think about such ones as The Polish Scouting Association, school self-governments, school sport clubs, sport centres and so forth.

Holiday and rehabilitation groups, youth camps are also an important forms of spending leisure time as participation in them brings compensation for existing deficiencies, increases metabolism, contributes to better social development and the ability of leading independent life, supports self-education, responsibility, resourcefulness and develops interests. The results of participating in such well-organized holiday activities are easily noticeable. Experiences obtained in this way may increase the pace of

> physical as well emotional and social development. By taking part in such forms of relaxation children and young people may positively change their eating and hygienic habits and, as a result, obtain better general health condition (*ibidem*, p. 83).

What is more, they are provided with professional health care, appropriate equipment, a carefully planned educational and therapeutic program.

Due to their accessibility mass media also play a significant role in managing leisure time of the mentally handicapped children and young people. They have a great impact on the charges who shape their views, models of behaviour, enrich their knowledge and creativity, derive pleasure and joy.

> However, the power of mass media may differ. On the one hand it depends on the attractiveness and perception of a form (a film, a book, a programme), on the other hand it is influenced by an individual's attitude, interests and perception ability (*ibidem*, p. 84).

Radio and television create favourable conditions for familiarizing with music, arts, theatre and film. For many handicapped music is not only an interesting way of spending their leisure time, but also an artistic expression. Programmes on social, political or cultural subject as well as scientific and educational ones may provide knowledge that makes exploring various issues and phenomena possible. By describing events and presenting interesting characters they help broaden minds and compare things and people.

Another attractive form of spending free time is attending events organized by cultural facilities. Visiting museums, concert halls, theatres and operas is an activity popular with the charges. The effects of these institutions depend upon their equipment, attractiveness of the offer and, first of all, accessibility.

Educational culture of the parents is very important, thus. The good of their child is the most important to them and this approach makes keeping contact with culture easier, creates favourable educational situations so the child can take part in cultural events on his own.

Social life is an inseparable part of spending leisure time. All social activities develop in the family as well as at a school, a club, a work place, wherever children and young people meet other people and socialize with them.

Social life has a special meaning as

it satisfies the needs for friendship, activeness, entertainment as well as realizes educational and rehabilitation goals such as: shaping the skills in behaving in different situations/places, mixing with other people, developing interpersonal skills, overcoming worries and fears, forming personal culture (Ploch, 1992, p. 85).

The above forms of spending leisure time may be applied at schools and outside them by professional educators, parents, tutors or volunteers.

Appropriately organized free time favours of human development in different spheres: a cognitive sphere as well as personal, social and physical ones. Leisure plays an important role in the rehabilitation of the mentally handicapped. Its main goal and task is to increase

maximum skills in performing basic activities, preparing for professional life, creating favourable conditions for mixing with natural and social environment (Parchomiuk, 2000, p. 13).

Leisure time shall have a special role in the mentally handicapped people's lives as it supports rehabilitation program and integrates the single elements of the rehabilitation system.

References

Łobożewicz T., Bińczyk G., *Podstawy turystyki*, Warszawa 2001.

Parchomiuk M., S*posoby spędzania czasu wolnego przez młodzież upośledzoną umysłowo w stopniu lekkim i sprawną umysłowo*, „Wychowanie na co dzień" 2000, kwiecień, 4–5.

Pięta J., *Pedagogika czasu wolnego*, Warszawa 2004.

Ploch L., *Jak organizować czas wolny dzieci i młodzieży upośledzonych umysłowo*, Warszawa 1992.

Iwona
Rudek

Difficulties of growing up
Educational dilemmas
that teachers and parents are facing

It is safe to say that both home and school constitute major educational setting for upbringing. Family as the first and the most powerful core representative of social life imposes decisive and at the same time characteristic influence on the life of a young adult. This is because the interrelation, educationally speaking, occurs continually and imperturbably in, usually, stable yet dynamic environment while involving true every day, informal and spontaneous situations. School, however, happens to be a place where upbringing occurs in more formal and institutionalized setting. Nowadays educational interrelations mean aid in development; such stand enables symmetric and based on partnership treatment of people in educational relations. In modern education single person individual way is particularly emphasized which leads to paying attention to the need of changing the organization of action taken up by teachers of reformed or still reforming school. In the light of the above, it is advisable to put student with their development in the middle of the educational setting. Moving the point of interest from the schooling onto the student is to getting to individualize the process of teaching and learning. Quality, integral assumption of knowledge and individualized approach to students become priority in the well organized school. Such priorities make people look back and set new guidelines for educating the generation of youngsters in this changing world.

School as a place helping facilitating
young people's development

The process of education occurring at school is one of the most important tasks for teachers-educators. Educator's work with growing up teenagers is a kind of test of being competent in the area of development support and personality mould of their students. People who grow up have specific expectations from the social groups they belong to. It indicates the need of taking up the tasks which shape their autonomy and their character. It is worth remembering that the need evolves from experiencing self-esteem built on acceptation arising from teachers and peers. Teachers, then, working with growing up teenagers have the knowledge of quite common principle, namely: As a student becomes more self-esteemed, and gains the knowledge of the rules their expectations are based on, they rebel against such tenet and consequently feel the burden of the imperatives they are bound to listen to without any chance to disobey it.

> If one listens to their elders only because those have rewards, then in adolescent period one understands the actions inspired by teachers, school or regulations.

Mastering the mechanism of growing up period and its influence on evolving teenager is a challenge both for a professional educator and often unaware yet loving parent. It might explain the overall difficulties concerning growing up period. This distinctive, colourful and natural period in the proper development of human beings is unfortunately often seen as negative and difficult.

Student – teacher relationship

The aim of the above presented deliberations is to focus the attention on specific kind of interaction between students and their teachers and then on the use of appropriate technique teachers utilise on the maturing teenagers. Analysing the literature of investigated subject matters one might assume that:

> A competent teacher has [...] vast knowledge of the subject, pedagogic skills, is professional – reflexive, sensible and reliable. While knowing pedagogical and educational methods 'such understanding of teacher's competence gives rise to further deliberation.

Dialogue which is usually understood as a form of specific cooperation between a student and a teacher is one of the fundamental rules in the area of interpersonal activities amongst growing up teenagers. School is such an institution where, by definition, the process of dialoguing should appear and be cultivated both by teachers and students. Yet, to make it feasible several conditions must be met. Being able to communicate i.e.; stating the point of view, defending this point of view, readiness to listen to the point of view of others, resolving conflicts are among others. Thus, proper, facilitating development, pedagogical and counselling actions which are all taken up by educators should be marked by:
– subject instead of object in student v. teacher correlation;
– treating students as growing up not grown up which means being understanding and tolerant;

- knowledge of the specific difficulties which characterise growing up period and awareness of changes taking place in various stages of life;
- getting to know students, collecting information about their behaviour, while being pedagogically alert revising this information;
- real cooperation with the parents based on systematic contact and both sides involvement in the process of development of students;
- true willingness to create proper conditions and readiness to help in student development;
- unconditioned acceptation of a student, perceiving them as someone having potential, whose evolution results from teacher's action and proper atmosphere of their development;
- giving and respecting the right to choose especially when it comes to deciding about future prospects.

Being a teenager's parent

Family, as the primal educational setting, have crucial and lasting influence on personality development. The time when children grow up happens to be a difficult time for parents who cannot confront the problem of being unable to: 'catch up with a child who passes the time we live in and enters their own time which means future'. Time for many parents begins to elapse so quickly and everything in a child changes that one time they are surprised to realize that their own child who appears before their eyes has become an almost developed young adult. Development unfortunately happens to be irregular and does not concern all the areas at once. A person who is a grown up physically is not usually developed socially, intellectually or emotionally.

Many people while becoming parents forget about being humans and that makes raising children difficult. The most important parents' role in the process of bringing up children is their readiness to be helpful and understanding and being in a position to create optimal educational setting in the home environment. In such environment a child is able to build up, just like in a puzzle, their own personality traits, individuality, self-esteem or skill in seeking their own place in life. It is also worth mentioning that teenager's independence is, by many parents, seen as reclusion or rejection. This may lead to frustration and misunderstanding. In reality, however, children do need their parents and what only changes, is the way they interrelate.

Adults, especially parents should first and foremost try to understand the growing child. Understand means being able to provide a spectrum of virtues to be followed which might help young person to build their independence, autonomy and inner freedom on. While building up the right relation the awareness of certain behaviour might come in use. The behaviour towards a child is based on the following principles: acceptation, loyalty, respecting privacy, equality, stability, consequence, request, co-decision and last but not least humour. Young people value such attitude of their parents which is characterised by: being able to perceive them as responsible partners who are ready for foresight thinking, critical assessment of their behaviour and what is more treating them equally while allowing them to partake in important family decision making.

In order to make a teenager create a good self picture important thing is to enhance the strong sides of a teenager which later influences the process of shaping their autonomy.

Instead of summing up

Educational problems parents and teachers have to deal with during puberty time make this puberty time be known as the time of crisis, conflict, rebellion, disintegration or negativism. The researchers who deal with the problem professionally claim that putting it in such light might contribute to fossilizing the negative picture of it. In reality, however, the time of puberty is believed to be important and valuable both for parents and educators alike. In spite of all difficulties and hard time it brings, it is the time of personality development and character shaping. The period in life which occurs during puberty is known as positive features stage – features which influence development and maturity of man. Assuming this fact one must put a lot of pressure on arising parental consciousness and on teachers reflecting thinking just in order to make students aware of this specific period of growing up. It is strongly advisable to support teenagers in surpassing problems so that they could evolve well.

References

Biblioteczka reformy. Ministerstwo Edukacji Narodowej o wychowaniu w szkole, MEN Biuro Administracyjno-Gospodarcze, Warszawa 1999.

Faber A., Mazlish E., *Jak mówić, żeby dzieci nas słuchały. Jak słuchać, żeby dzieci do nas mówiły*, przeł. M. Więznowska, Poznań 1993.

Gordon T., *Wychowanie bez porażek*, przeł. A. Makowska, E. Sujak, Warszawa 1991.

Hamer H., *Klucz do efektywności nauczania*, Warszawa 1994.

Jabłońska M. (red.), *Nauczyciel w zmieniającej się rzeczywistości społecznej*, Wrocław 2000.

Jaczewski A., Woynarowska B. (red.), *Dojrzewanie*, Warszawa 1982.

Koć-Seniuch G., Cichocki A. (red.), *Nauczyciel i uczniowie w dyskursie edukacyjnym*, Białystok 2000.

Mastalski J., *Samotność globalnego nastolatka*, Kraków 2007.

Płócińska M., Rylce H., *Czas współpracy i czas zmian*, Warszawa 2002.
Przetacznik-Gierowska M., Włodarski Z., *Psychologia wychowawcza*, Warszawa 1994.
Rubacha K. (red.), *Wokół szkoły i edukacji. Syntezy i refleksje*, Toruń 1997.
Rylke H., *Pokolenie zmian. Czego boją się dorośli?*, Warszawa 1999.

Aldona
Molesztak

Contemporary problems in bringing up children

Introduction

The society often treats the process of bringing up a child as a simple task. Parents, basing on their own childhood experiences, attempt to reproduce the educational methods they were subject to. However, generations differ due to the variety of stimuli provided by the developing civilisation. By means of television programs the mass media try to assist parents providing them with the knowledge they can take advantage of while rearing their child. Unfortunately, facing difficulties, parents fail to observe their own deficiencies or mistakes made in the upbringing process. The fact that parents brought up in other circumstances and for different future have to prepare young generation for their life in conditions they could not expect (Brzezińska, 1999). The academic community should concentrate on proposing wide-ranging emergency and long-term assistance in solving a variety of upbringing problems. Only then, parents and teachers prepared for the process beforehand will raise the new generation in accordance with the human development cycle. As characteristic features of the process are its duration and continuity, the long-term goal should be consistently and persistently followed. Parents, however, often miss to discern problems rising from family itself and tend to seek help in treatment of results, not in identification of the actual cause of child's misbehaviour.

Sources of problems in child rearing

Every child is observed to misbehave from time to time, and that is a natural characteristic of childhood and adolescence periods. Children learn to function in their families, in the society or group by gathering good and bad experiences, testing to find limits to which they can act without restraints towards their parents, teachers or other children. When the first symptoms of misbehaviour occur is difficult to establish (Kołakowski, 2007, p. 110). The present article will discuss a few approaches analysing causes of problem behaviour. Irrespectively of the year of the publication its discussion of child's misconduct causes remains relevant. Moreover, new questions are continued to appear as a result of the civilisation development.

Manifold origins for upbringing problems occurrence and entrenchment have been described in literature, but the most widely accepted division includes exogenic and endogenic causes discovered in changed development factors and their complex interdependencies. As follows from the above, the explicit influence of particular factors is difficult to be precisely identified since it depends on e.g. external conditions, the child itself, his/her age, experiences, sensitivity, the way his/her nervous system works, on living conditions of the family, on the system of demands, applied parenting methods, behaviour patterns, on single-occurrence situations and events all contributing to creation of the unique network of individual causes and factors facilitating appearance of misbehaviour. It is essential to determine the child's sensitivity, his/her way of reacting to stimuli, resistance to failure and frustration, tolerance to command, bans or restrictions. Children's emotions towards safety, care and independence are different from those of adults (Kaja, 1972). That trend of research has appeared in numerous publications since it reflects on such sources as the child itself or the society and includes psychologization, as well as socialization and pedagogization distinguished by Otto Speck (2007).

Considering upbringing problems one may find that they originate from:
1) incompatibility between parenting methods and education at nursery school or kindergarten;
2) mistakes parents make;
3) upbringing styles preferred by parents;
4) disturbances of the development process (temperament and personality);
5) inability to identify stages in child development.

A child starts shaping his/her social behaviour influenced by upbringing methods used by their parents and the environment. Thus, the child's conduct depends on

> how parents establish and implement rules, support and encourage the child and exert their authority, how they structuralize their child's life and make it predictable (Vasta, Haith, Miller, 1995, p. 472, own translation).

Parents approach the undertaking in a variety of ways. Unfortunately, the educational institution often performs its task in a manner unlike that used by the family environment and as a result the child faces a situation of a cognitive dissonance – incompatibility of two concepts. Thus, the child has to substantiate his/her choice of one idea as a rule of conduct or may develop and integrate a conviction that behaviour depends on the current environment. The latter situation often results in problems arising in both upbringing environments and may lead to the child developing neurosis.

Irena Obuchowska (1976) distinguishes the following interfering features of the environment:

a) considerable inconsistence in demands (e.g. a child is always assisted at home, while at kindergarten is expected to act unaided),

b) mutually contradictory demands leading to a situation where a child is praised or punished for the same conduct (e.g. praised for being curious at kindergarten but punished for persistence in asking questions at home),

c) the fact that demand are not adjusted to the child's abilities.

High demands have a traumatic influence on children and the too low ones may result in neurosis by lowering the psychic immunity (a child accustomed to success at home is not capable of accepting failure). Marta Bogdanowicz writes about the difficulty in identification of one neurosis source because the disorder is caused by a chain of numerous phenomena.

> Children are particularly exposed to the risk of developing neurotic disorders as their nervous system is immature, and their acquired mechanism of coping with difficult situations is not sufficiently strong (Bogdanowicz, 1991, p. 181, own translation).

Preferred parenting styles determine the method of task realisation. Before characterising the styles of upbringing in detail, let me quote Halina Spionek (1963) who pointed to upbringing problems while describing infants. Though published years ago Spionek's statements perfectly exemplify contemporary parents. The symptoms of upbringing problems include so called 'whims' and negative emotional states most often resulting from mistakes made in the upbringing process in family or at nursery. The author blames such disruption of the daily schedule of the family as changed the sleep or meal time, rocking, too much amusement just before bedtime, telling stories or scaring, which may cause sleep disorders and, consequently, to chronic fatigue of the nervous system manifesting with overexcitement or crying for trivial reasons. The overall irritation may also follow from overheating, uncomfortable or too tight clothes or actions of parents wishing to do something too quickly what results in their child developing e.g. a fear of bath, getting dressed or meals. Failure to observe one's own mistakes in the upbringing process as surrendering to whims or acting 'in defiance' leads to children developing multiple-symptom neurosis. Rearing a child is not a simple task; it means incessant work of the child and parents due to which the child's behaviour will comply with the social and moral norms.

One may further consider the distinguished by H. Spionek degrees of deficient upbringing resulting from the parent-child relationship. There is no parent who could avoid some failure or oversight in the process of upbringing a child i.e. a parental mistake. As a result of the child rearing process parents can be found to bring up their children well, badly or disastrously. The first level of deficient upbringing is characteristic for children in the first years of life when only minor mistakes are observed. Parents lavish affection, attention and care on their child, however, with time they fail to attend to some spheres of child's psychical development. The second stage is observed later in the child's life, when the scope and intensity of parental mistakes prevent socially-accepted behaviour in majority of everyday situations. The mono- or bidirectional parent-child relationship becomes deteriorated. The third level means that parents lose contact with the child entirely, resigning from their influence, or act ineffectively (Spionek, 1981, pp. 56–57). The discussed stages may be compared to the process of creating a unique upbringing environment determined by mistakes made by parents.

There is no coherence in descriptions of parenting styles found in literature but those most often proposed are described as: 1) autocratic, 2) liberal, 3) democratic, and 4) inconsistent. H. Spionek (1963) lists the following deficient parenting styles: over-strict and rigorous (coercive), over-indulging and inconsistent. However, one may accept as the best the division into four following types: autocratic (authoritarian), uninvolved, permissive and authoritative (Vasta, Haith, Miller, 1995).

Parents preferring the autocratic upbringing style are extremely demanding, supervise and control their children incessantly enforcing their demands with threats and punishment. Children react badly to the style showing discontent in relationships, moodiness, aggression and disobedience. Another style, the uninvolved one, imposes few limits but offers children little care, attention or emotional support. As a consequence, indifferent parents contribute to their children developing excessive demands and disobedience. Disturbed social relations and no effective participation in play are observed. The permissive style means permission for a child 'to do anything'. Parents adopting this upbringing style tend to be very affectionate and emotionally sensitive, imposing few restrictions on the child. On one hand, the parents motivate their children to behave properly by means of their acceptance and encouragement, on the other, they offer little assistance to their child trying to structuralize the predictability of the environment. As a result, children of permissive parents act similarly to children reared in the autocratic style, showing frequent impulsiveness, immaturity and being incontrollable. The fourth discussed parenting style, the authoritative one, is perceived as the most advantageous and is employed by parents characterised as protective and sensitive to children's needs. Children are to observe clear and understandable limits and rules; consistency and responsibility are other features of the style. Children brought up by authoritative parents are curios, confident and independent (Vasta, Haith, Miller, 1995; Obuchowska, 2004).

Contemporary research has shown that a system of upbringing practices understood as a responsible procedure determines the development and autonomy of a child. O. Speck provides the following definition s of the concepts:

1) neither the authoritarian nor the permissive upbringing style is conducive to the process of a child becoming an autonomic individual;
2) dependency, apathy, aggressiveness may follow from prevalence of instructional practices;
3) overindulgence of caregivers may encourage children's aggression, tyranny and wilfulness;
4) good conditions for the development of child's autonomy are observed when the parenting style bases on the stable emotional bonds and sympathetic interest, when, thanks to reciprocal communication, the child is influenced by clearly expressed norms and supportive control, when the caregivers' actions are adapted to the developmental stage of the child, i.e. the more independent the child grows the more restraint in using upbringing practices is observed on the part of the parent; in other words, the caregiver's trust constitutes encouragement and support for the child in his/her passing from one independence level to another (Speck, 2007, p. 244, own translation).

Temperament may be another source of problems in the upbringing process. The interpretation has not been substantiated, though so called 'difficult children' are recognised to be in the risk group because of the greater probability of behaviour disorders. Unfortunately, the influence mechanism remains unexplained. For example, shy children show an early temperamental feature, namely inhibition observed in their behaviour in early childhood and remaining stable for a number of years. Some research has pointed out that the feature may change with time. Moreover, shyness, bashfulness and so called difficult temperament may be interrelated with experience and socialisation (Vasta, Haith, Miller, 1995).

Subject literature describes child's personality development as at least parallel to the general physical and psychic progress. However, one should stress the fact that the process is not unambiguous as

there is no definite answer to the question if the maturation process of all organism functions and psyche is of the same importance for individual development or if the process strictly depends on the type of those functions (Chłopkiewicz, 1987, p. 157).

Though all functional capabilities of an individual are reflected in the child's personality some of them are particularly stressed. M. Chłopkiewicz (*ibidem*, p. 302) writes that

Developmental process disorders leading to permanent deformations, inhibitions and retardations in formation of the personal structure are a specifically childhood problem. Those are the source of the considerable number of upbringing difficulties and the cause of limited effectiveness of parenting influence. They initiate the process of wide-ranging deformations of an adult personality, and contribute to emergence of neurotic or sociopathological disorders.

Child's behaviour follows some patterns and is highly in a predictable, i.e. the biological and psychic development of a child progresses according to a specific outline. Thus, human behaviour is subject to a number of set rules and norms (Ilig, Ames, Baker, 2006). Innate predisposition of a child and characteristics of the developmental stage she/he has reached influence the behaviour to not lesser extent than the way the child is treated by parents and the environment. Child's behaviour depends not only on his/her developmental stage but also on his/her former experiences of relations within the family and the environment. Parents should learn to recognise the natural behaviour of their children since the child's development is compatible with the distribution of balance and imbalance periods over the developmental scheme. Therefore, if the child's behaviour suddenly changes one should not seek reasons for the transformation in the child's background or his/her difficult character. Periods of balance, both internal and in relations with people and the external world, are intertwined with periods when the child does not feel comfortable even with him/herself and seems to be in conflict with other people. What is essential is the sequence of those periods as very child imposes her/his own pace on the series but every stage of comparative balance is followed by a period of unrest and unadjustedness. Adults should realise that every stage in the child's development has both positive and negative.

Literature specifies other causes for upbringing problems originating from the following domains:

1. Misbehaviour as a consequence of a variety of symptoms – the 'difficult' conduct is a result of symptoms of disorders or diseases (e.g. delirium caused by high temperature), or emotional problems. Often the child is unable to control appearance or disappearance of the specific behaviour.
2. Unfamiliarity with the rules – the misbehaviour is accepted by its environment irrespectively of the child's compliance to the rules or expectations.
3. Misbehaviour – connected with conscious activity of a child who is aware of rules and norms but violates them to achieve something or to test parental determination.
4. Impulsive aggression occurring most often when a child cannot cope with the situation he/she faces or in a state of strong emotional tension and shows as a sudden outburst.
5. Socialised aggression where a child of low internal excitability tries to hide the fact and escape consequence. The aggression is connected with gains and many a time is combined with occurrence of major behavioural disorders.
6. Oppositional and noncompliant behaviour – negativist, hostile, rebellious, provocative and destructive behaviour transgressing norms accepted for the age and socio-cultural context.
7. Major (serious) behaviour disorders – consciously violating other people's rights and socially accepted norms (Kołakowski, Wolańczyk, Pisula, Skotnicka, Bryńska, 207, pp. 109–110).

The analysed behaviour is a result of the child's relations with parents and surroundings. Diagram 1 presents a model according to which the child's behaviour forms. It points out to the fact that parents devoid of knowledge, imagination and, primarily, consistency by their upbringing practises contributes to the occurrence of misbehaviour. Parents should react to such behaviour calmly, determining reasons for child's emotions, but at the same time also outwardly expressing their disapproval. The child should have a chance to think over the misbehaviour as only in this way he/she is given an opportunity to learn to solve problems in the future relying on communication and feeling responsibility for his/her own conduct. Thus, the child has to learn the rules and norms of functioning within the society. If parents are indulgent to undesirable behaviour or if they fail to react to it at all, the child will fail to discover and integrate the rules and norms. Similarly, if parents overreact shouting or being aggressive, the child will learn to solve the problems in the same way, namely, with aggression. Parents have to react to every occurrence of misbehaviour as only in this way they prevent the child from entrenching the behaviour. If the reaction fails to occur, it may be interpreted as a reward. The upbringing process and all activities within must be continuous, not sporadic. The parents' behaviour described above presents a model of shaping child's behaviour presented in an article on ADHD and shows the scheme of child' behaviour in a simple way.

Diagram 1. Model of child's behaviour shaping

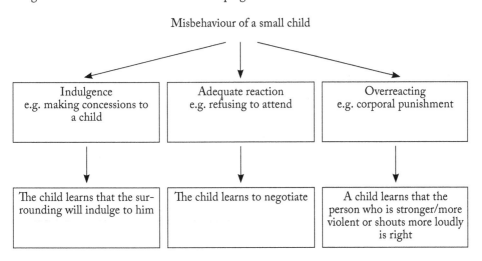

Source: Kołakowski, Wolańczyk, Pisula, Skotnicka, Bryńska, 2007, p. 111.

It follows from the process that the misbehaviour occurs and becomes entrenched as a result of parents' beliefs systems. The systems are clear-cut and precise but parents very often fail to apply them to problems appearing in everyday situations. The assumptions may also be invalid altogether and lead to improper upbringing practises as in the case of the uninvolved style. The model below presents parenting practices resulting in changes in child's conduct. The system of interactions is explained by H. R. Schaffer.

Diagram 2. Interactions between the system of parental belief, their parental practices and child's development

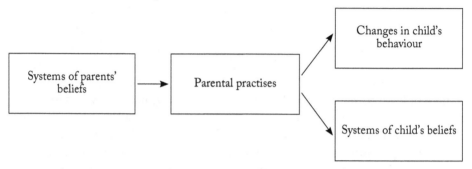

Source: Schaffer, 2008, p. 55.

The system suggests that parents' systems of beliefs do not directly influence children but influence adults' behaviour towards children. As follows, the implementation occurs in upbringing practices employed by parents.

It is those practises that impinge children's behaviour and, therefore, the beliefs system that they are going to develop later on (Schaffer, 2008, p. 54).

In the Reuven Feuerstein's concept of mediated learning used by A. Brzezińska the caregiver is a mediator between a child and the environment. An effective mediator is a person whose behaviour is a well-organized entity, is consistent and reasonable. The caregiver acts in a flexible way adjusting and diversifying methods of drawing attention to himself depending on the child's behaviour. The adult tries to 'explain' the reality to the child, the reality they both participate in, i.e. comments on objects, activities and events occurring around them. In a competent manner the parent expresses his/her emotions evoked by the child's behaviour and tries to establish relations with the child, if is possible, also maintaining eye contact. Moreover, the adult concentrates on actions, statements and child's questions. The child should be encouraged, directed towards specific ways of behaviour and should not just act on orders. The caregiver structures expectations of the child towards the situation to follow by means of various statements. The child should receive some reward while acting. It is essential to make all accidental behaviour of the child a reasonable cause and effect sequence (Brzezińska, Janiszewska-Rain, 2005).

Parents, taking advantage of the upbringing guidelines above, may check the child's behaviour against the model described in *Dziecko ryzyka a wychowanie. Elementarz dla rodziców* [*A risk child and upbringing. The ABC for parents*] by E. M. Minczakiwicz (2005) which provides adults with procedures for their work with their children as well as observation forms. It is an interesting handbook corresponding to the presented child rearing problems.

A child establishing accurate relations with adults is capable of self-regulation i.e. the internalised skill of adjusting his/her emotions, comments and behaviour in response to internal and external stimuli. J. Wojciechowska points out that early childhood achievements are the basis for competencies needed later on, at school, and describes the self-regulation skill as concerning: postponement of gratification, inhibition of impulsive reaction and an organised task-based action. The aspects mentioned above form the basis of social, emotional and cognitive development of the child through subsequent stages. Thus, what seems important is the influence method, adult's control over the child's behaviour, introduction to social life standards into the child's experience, diversification of behaviour and emotions (frequently negative ones). She continues to state that dangers following from the developmental stage for the process of self-control mechanism formation are associated with three basic risk areas according to Kopp (1982, 1989). The risk areas encompass child's temperamental features, the quality of parenting practises and are associated with cognitive and linguistic competencies as the foundation for communication of the child with adults and for control over his/her own experience. The potential of the child and ways of developing the child's competence by adults by everyday stimulation are of major importance. At the same time one should not forget that self-regulation depends on the development of such functions as the problem-solving skill, memory and speech. Cognitive and language development deficiencies very often accompany children's aggressive behaviour and hyperactivity (Wojciechowska, 2005).

In conclusion, the formed beliefs systems are the basis for applied parenting practice contributing not only to initiating specific ways of conduct but to a child forming his/her own belief system. Thus, a simple scheme arises.

Discussing the contemporary approach to difficulties O. Speck points out that the problems arise as a result of 'de-anchoring processes, i.e. disintegration of bonds in the increasingly differentiating society' (Speck, 2007, p. 62). The process is extremely hazardous as in the situation of 'differentiating functional systems disorders of ecological resonance may arise i.e. a limited ability of an individual to react accurately to external interference' (*ibidem*, p. 63). In the contemporary society, the 'society of risk', an individual yields to countless influences and dangers. A survey of the contemporary society of today has allowed researchers to form theories basing on a variety of assumptions associated with the occurrence of upbringing problems.

One of the theories concerns resigning from moral evaluation in an attempt to overcome the binding since the first half of the 20th c, moralist and repressive upbringing model and, consequently, to lift the moralist criterion in evaluation of 'child's mistakes'. At present the tendency of resigning from the moral dimension bases on the pluralism of norms (Speck, 2007).

The modern society is characterised by moral relativity understood in three ways: as cognitive relativism, ethic relativism and contextual relativism. However, Hanna Świda-Ziemba recognizes permissivism (indulgence), i.e. tolerance towards cases of breaking moral norms, as the most characteristic attitude of the Polish society.

> Permissivism is accompanied with abstract recognition of moral norms and social consent to their content being ascribed academic status'. Permissive people are characterised by the so called 'split' between the acceptance of norms and reaction to the acts of their breaking. The acceptance is abstract, and follows from other personality layer than the judgement of oneself and other people. The recognised norms do not constitute a prism through which one judges the reality (Świda-Ziemba, 2002, p. 438).

The contemporary world with its characteristics as deinstitutionalism, detraditionalism, pluralism and individualism favours such values as: autonomy of making decisions, self-realization and faith in progress. Long-term goals are abandoned in favour of specific aims (Mariański, 2006). All those reflections allow a conclusion that the contemporary crisis is being deepened.

Medicalization is another theory of difficulty origin understood as an attempt to penetrate the core of the child's misbehaviour by including the behaviour into the pathology or disease domain. Apparently, recognition of misbehaviour as a disease entails relieving the moral burden from individuals and results in the described above relativity of ethic values. In conclusion one should stress that reducing all solutions of upbringing problems to prescribing medicine is irresponsible since one may not reduce all problems to disease only as it will limit the scope of problem examination. Psychologization aims at explaining child's misbehaviour by means of psychological phenomena while sociologization finds causes for misconduct in specific socialisation processes within the framework of the society. The pathogenic influence of the environment on the child calls for transformation of social relations, improvement of living conditions in lowest community layers, etc. Pedagogization overstresses the rules of responsiveness and support. According to that theory a child poses a difficult object for upbringing and therapy for parents (Speck, 2007). The above theories tend to analyse only one aspect of the problem of misbehaviour what, according to O. Speck, does not allow an overall view of the question.

Conclusion

A child cannot be separated from the family and the environment. The family creates social development conditions and shapes the child's life. The child's progress and the emotional state of the child are interrelated with the conditions and atmosphere within the family. Parents in their relations with children test their parental beliefs. If parents make mistakes following from inadequate reaction to a situation or failing to identify causes for child's misbehaviour, change rules and demands or are inconsistent, they cause occurrence or entrenchment of the child's misconduct. A small child shows little sign of misbehaviour that could be entrenched by parental practises. Children misbehave because parents have problems. Not only were parents brought up in different conditions but also they are unprepared for their role of caregivers. The child's behaviour reflects rules and norms set by parents.

Contemporary parents enumerate the following problems with their children: child's negativism, hyperactivity, aggression, timidity, jealousy, nutrition problems, dependence (or rather lack of independence), early age masturbation, lying, egoism (Obuchowska, 2004). Child's behaviour may be characterised as imitative or defensive, may be a cry for help or an attempt to draw attention.

First discipline problems should signal to parents the need for correction of heir own attitude. Unfortunately, even sensible parents surrender to whims or act defiantly thus intensifying the child's misbehaviour. In this way a situation of the vicious circle occurs:

> as a consequence of child's misbehaviour resulting from deficient parental approach, mistakes made by parents in the upbringing process multiply, leading to even more serious problems. The situation is the more dangerous that a small child easily forms habits, incorrect stereotypes and practices harmful for his/her further development (Spionek, 1963, pp. 344–345).

It is their parents who have to decide on priorities, have to choose between professional careers, high salary and time spent with their children, between a temporarily incomplete family as a result of immigration for economic purposes (a child in such a family is referred to as a euro-orphan) and life in poorer conditions but together, between separation or divorce and living together for proper development of the child. Disabled parents of disabled children face even more dilemmas. One should not forget pathologic families and those living in poverty.

Knowledge of what one may face does not mean that one is exempt from the duty of opposing misbehaviour. But the knowledge may help parents fight it more effectively than if they faced the problem empty-handed. Thus, there are situations when misbehaviour ought to be replaced with more proper conduct, in some cases it is enough to counteract, in other one has to face the challenge and struggle.

Translating Joanna Górzyńska

References

Bogdanowicz M., *Psychologia kliniczna dziecka w wieku przedszkolnym*, Warszawa 1991.

Brzezińska A., *Edukacja wobec wyzwań społeczności lokalnych* [w:] H. Sęk, S. Kowalik (red.), *Psychologiczny kontekst problemów społecznych*, Poznań 1999.

Brzezińska A., Janiszewska-Rain J., *W poszukiwaniu złotego środka*, Kraków 2005.

Chłopkiewicz M., *Osobowość dzieci i młodzieży. Rozwój i patologia*, Warszawa 1987.

Ilg F. L., *Rozwój psychiczny dziecka od 0 do 10 lat*, Gdańsk 2006.

Ilg F. L., Ames L. B., Baker S. M., *Rozwój psychiczny dziecka od 0 do 10 lat*, przeł. M. Przylipiak, Gdańsk 2006.

Kaja H., *Trudności wychowawcze wieku szkolnego*, Bydgoszcz 1972.

Kołakowski A., Wolańczyk T., Pisula A., Skotnicka M., Bryńska A., *ADHD – zespół nadpobudliwości psychoruchowej*, Gdańsk 2007.

Kopp C. B., *Antecedents of self-regulation: A developmental perspective*, 'Developmental Psychology' 1982, 18, 199–214.

Kopp C. B., *Regulation of distress and negative emotions. A developmental view*, 'Developmental Psychology' 1989, 25, 343–354.

Minczakiewicz E. M., Grzyb B., Gajewski Ł., *Dziecko ryzyka a wychowanie*, Kraków 2005.

Obuchowska I., *Dynamika nerwic*, Warszawa 1976.

Obuchowska I., *Portret psychologiczny dzieci w wieku przedszkolnym, style rodzicielskiego wychowania i wychowawcze problemy* [w:] T. Ogrodzińska (red.), *Nigdy nie jest za wcześnie – rozwój i edukacja małych dzieci*, Warszawa 2004.

Schaffer H. R., *Psychologia dziecka*, przeł. A. Wojciechowski, Warszawa 2008.

Speck, *Trudności wychowawcze*, przeł. E. Cieślik, Gdańsk 2007.

Spionek H., *Rozwój i wychowanie małego dziecka*, Warszawa 1963.

Spionek H., *Zaburzenia rozwoju uczniów a niepowodzenia szkolne*, Warszawa 1981.

Tyszka Z., *Socjologia rodziny*, Warszawa 1974.

Vasta R., Haith M. M., Miller S. A., *Psychologia dziecka*, przeł. M. Babiuch, Warszawa 1995.

Wojciechowska J., *Wiek niemowlęcy. Jak rozpoznać ryzyko i jak pomagać* [w:] A. Brzezińska (red.), *Psychologiczne portrety człowieka*, Gdańsk 2005.

Ziemska M. (red.), *Rodzina i dziecko*, Warszawa 1980.

Part 2 Research report

Violetta
Kopińska

Contemporary problems of student council

Introduction

According to the simplest definition, referring to the semantic meaning of the polish word, a council means that a group of people govern on their own. The contemporary utility of such definition, in my view, is doubtful. Perceiving a student council as a form of government is not coherent with currently existing forms of student councils. However there is not any elaborate definition which embodies various sorts of school councils. What is common and what appears in all definitions of student council is a factor of social participation and socializing by empowering certain communities to make decisions (Kozioł, 2000, p. 39). Thus, a student council is connected with democracy, though not necessarily bigger democracy awarded in a process of empowerment. Tomasz Fuks (1995) believed that the only formal, valid criterion allowing to differentiate between councils is denominating the given organizations as councils by a legislator. In compliance with hierarchy of legal acts valid in The Republic of Poland, the legal foundation can be found in The Constitution of The Republic of Poland dated April 2, 1997 (Dz. U. z 1997 r. Nr 78, poz. 483). If we settle this in the context of a student council-the definition is provided in the Education System Act dated September 7, 1991 (Dz. U. z 2004 r. Nr 256, poz. 2572). The Article 55 of this Act defines a school council as a mandatory authority made of all the students of a particular school. The students in a secret ballot decide on the rules of the student council's general elections. Student council's authority represents the whole school community, while the representation is a result of a democratic entitlement. The main duties of the representatives are the following:
- expressing opinions of their classes-not their own opinions,
- responsibility towards the electorate-not for the electorate (Radziewicz, Mirgos, 1988, p. 53).

Article 55 of the Education System Act 5 specifies the competences of the student council. According to these regulations, a student council is entitled to present various motions and opinions concerning school to the school council, the teacher council or to the headmaster, especially the ones regarding the fundamental rights of students such as: the right to get accustomed with the curriculum and the expectations of the teachers, the right to proper assessment of the learning progress, the right to organize school life, enabling keeping the right balance between school effort and the ability to develop individual interests, the right to draft and issue school paper, the right to organize cultural, educational and sports events according to individual needs and organizational possibilities, in co-operation with the headmaster and finally the right to elect the teacher in charge of a student council. Therefore the only regulatory competence is the entitlement to establish the rules of the elections of the student council authorities. Other competences, including the ones connected with the implementation of students' rights, are expounded in a rather cautious way as the entitlement to present motions and opinions, which after all, are not always binding. Therefore, the main question that can be raised is, whether the student council really is a legislative organ or just a form of self-government typical of social life organisation? Regardless of the answer a student council exists as a social category and even pedagogical, though my impression is, that-real characteristics belonging to that category is far from the essence of student council activity. Although there are a lot of works in pedagogical literature concerning student council, the context of its functioning is changing all the time. One of the questions that come to my mind, in the twentieth anniversary of the III Republic of Poland is the question about a contemporary student council, which is a reflection of the democratization relationships at school understood as a social microcircuit. For these reasons I have resolved to have a closer look at contemporary student councils in order to diagnose potential problems, at the same time trying to set them in a contemporary contexts.

Methodological remarks

All results, conclusions and observations expounded in the present study are based on the research conducted in November and December 2008 in Toruń. In the survey took part 373 students (184 girls and 189 boys) from the public junior high schools. The research was carried out in 6 schools of different numerical force. The tool used was an anonymous questionnaire with open questions included, which enabled qualitative analysis of the collected empirical material. The respondents were the second and third year students with the average age of 14,7[1].

---

[1] Standard fluctuation 0,64.

Student council is not created by all students

One of the essential problems that needs to be dealt with at a start is the way a student council is perceived. Is a student council created by all students of the given school? Let me analyse students' responses in the questionnaire.

The very definition of a student council provides interesting observations. Not surprisingly, a notion of self-governing is confined here to the student council. It comes as a consequence of a place where the research has been carried out and the role the young people are assigned there. Another quite important factor was the title placed on the questionnaire ('students self-governing'), in spite of the fact that the very question was general and the council was not specified.

Only single responses communicate the sense of community of the type 'we', e.g.

'This means, we can decide on the forms of governing ourselves, our vote is important',

'We recognize what is good and what is bad ourselves',

'It is something we govern on our own'

There were just a few such responses, but it needs to be emphasized that its 'authors are not necessarily the members of class or school council authorities.

The majority of definitions coined by researchers depict the lack of identification with the student council. The prevailing explanation is that of the third party., e.g.

'They come to agreements on various school and students' matters',

'They do something for the good of school'

This is a common, 'usual' way of defining notions. (Whereas coming up with definitions using the first person plural)[2] is rather rare.

However when we put a question in a different way, i.e. 'Are you a member of a student council?' conclusions are less ambiguous. Over 88% of the respondents answered in a negative way. This result only supports the hypothesis that a student council is identified with its authorities. Therefore the next question that can be raised is about the way the authorities are elected and their role for the whole community of students.

Every fourth student does no know how student council's authorities are elected, among those who claim they know (51,74%) or they think they know (16,89%) nearly half (48,83%) is not able to describe the procedure resorting to general statements like: 'in a voting', or 'in elections'. Some students' responses are astounding. 5,7% of respondents that announce they know how the student council's authorities are elected underscore the huge interference of the teachers ('The tutor has decided', 'The teacher elects the student and he cannot refuse').

---

[2] This certainly reflects strong identification with each student's duty or the duties of the whole student community.

On the other hand 4,7% of these students in their answers point out that there is not anything like elections. They argue there is a kind of drawing or volunteering This can be illustrated by the following statement: 'you can be elected if you like' . It is worth mentioning that among those students who said they did not know how the students council authorities were elected were also the ones that had never participated in elections. They explained it in the following way: '... because in our school student council is not elected by students'.

The question arises hereof the possible interpretations of such statements-which by the way- are uttered by students of a few schools only, which gives a small percentage of the total number of respondents. Do such statement reflect the real situation or just show the ignorance of students? Or do they project a negative attitude towards the student council's activities ?

These questions definitely require further research.

The above results of the research show that the sense of democratic bestowal regarding the student council authorities is not necessarily obvious for students.

So, do they perceive a student council as a representative authority which represents their interests?

See the categories of statements presented in the below diagram on how students understand the term student council (Table 1).

Table 1. Categories of statements concerning understanding of the term student council[3]

Understanding of Student Council Functions						
Responses	Girls		Boys		Altogether	
	no.	%	no.	%	no.	%
Responses emphasizing the aspect of governing: a group of people who govern on their own	54	29,35	58	30,69	112	30,03
Responses emphasizing the aspect of representation: a group of people representing someone	25	13,59	18	9,52	43	11,53
Responses emphasizing the supportive function of a student council: a group of people who help other students	20	10,87	10	5,29	30	8,04
General statements: a group of people who deal with class and school matters	22	11,96	22	11,64	44	11,80

The high proportion (11,8%) of the respondents provide a very general definition of the term, which makes it impossible to draw any conclusions on the functions assigned to a student council. More than 8% tend to assign the role of acting in students' interest, whereas more than 11% underscore the aspect of

---

[3] Categories hale been created on the basis of qualitative analysis of students' responses. It has been found out that one person did not give more than two answers.

representation. The most frequent definition of a student council refers to it's etymological meaning.

Let me now settle these general definitions in the contexts of the given schools in order to find some elements of representation and acting in students' interest in the responses given by students about the student councils in their schools.

For questions regarding student council's activity only 12,61% students out of 61,66% of the total number of respondents emphasized that student council decides on some school matters. However it is not specified whether the decisions are reached on behalf of the students, for them or in their interest. There were only a few mentions of a representative role of a student council.

Although the work of a student council is evaluated positively by more than 38% of the respondents, only less than 5% justify it by the student council's activities in the school's interest. One fourth of the respondents believe the student council in their school is necessary.

To summarize, representation of students' interests by a student council, which I believe is it's inherent feature, (next to a democratic bestowal) is not emphasized by students. Is not it important for them? This question cannot be answered explicitly yet. Let me analyze another opening of the research.

A student council 'governs on it's own – students know nothing about it'

Another problem, closely linked with the lack of democratic foundation, and not enough emphasized function of representation of students interest, is perceiving a student council as an isolated or isolating group. The following statements are characteristic of such perception:

'I have no insight into what is going on in the student council...'.

'None of the student council's initiatives refer to me...'.

Within the discussed problem we can raise a few specific issues such as:
a) elitism of student council authorities,
b) students' ignorance of the school authorities structure,
c) trust to the student council authorities.

Unfortunately all the above mentioned issues are clearly visible in all the negative responses, statements and opinions of the students who took part in the survey on how they perceive a student council in their schools. Statements in which a student council is depicted as a closed group of students are provided while giving the definition or justification for the lack of knowledge about student council activities or the elections procedure.

Characteristic can be an opinion hold by a 14 year old student, who defined the student council in the following way: 'it is electing someone to be a better student'.

When it comes to students' ignorance, I would like to underscore a wrong conviction that teachers belong to a student council. It is difficult to say whether this conviction of the respondents results from their lack of knowledge of the structure of this body or rather from the actual involvement of teachers in student council activities. The latter I acknowledge to be true. The analysis of the questionnaire makes it possible to draw a conclusion that students are convinced of the actual and even authoritative role of the teachers. This can be a consequence of either the lack of knowledge on the part of the students or their lack of involvement in school activities. It is worth mentioning that some convictions can be further reflected in the assessment of a given situation. The respondents convictions on the active participation of the teachers in student council activities (resulting either from wrong conviction or from observations on the actual situation) leads to a negative evaluation of the student council and in consequence to questioning the need for it to exist at all[4].

The following statements provided by the respondents can illustrate the outlined earlier observations:

(I don't know what the student council in my school deals with)[5], because all is done by teachers'.

'A Student Council is made of students and teachers who implement both students and teachers ideas and inform everyone about it'.

(I am not a member of a student council and I am not interested to become one), because all in all students cannot decide about anything'.

There is a correlation between our perception of the student council and confidence we place in it. The lack of confidence can be the reason or the result of student council isolation. It is expressed mainly in negative statements about student council as non representative body.

This proves however that at least for some of the respondents representation of students interest still is an inherent feature of a student council.

We can divide the statements about the lack of fulfillment of its duties by the student council into:

     a) objective-when the actual situation makes making decisions impossible,

     b) subjective- associated with bad evaluation of the students deeds or even blaming them for the given situation.

The latter point of view can be illustrated with bitter remarks referring to student councils activity, e.g.:

---

[4] None of the respondents, who in their statements referred to students inability to make decisions and authoritative role of the teachers evaluated the student council positively (responses: *I don't hold any opinion, rather negatively/negatively*) or saw the need for it to exist (responses: *I don't know, rather not, no*).

[5] Author's remark.

'A few students who promise a lot and later do not keep their promises or only to some extent'.

'They deal with everything except for what is necessary'.

'The people who settle some matters in a way which I do not like'.

One indicator of the lack of confidence in what the student council does is the evaluation of the legitimacy of its existence (Table 2).

Table 2. Evaluation of the need for the student council to function at school

Is the Student Council Needed At School?					
Responses	Girls		Boys		Altogether	
	no.	%	no.	%	no.	%
Yes	75	40,76	48	25,40	123	32,98
I think so	48	26,09	49	25,92	97	26,01
I don't know	37	20,11	47	24,87	84	22,52
Not really	7	3,80	13	6,88	20	5,36
No	11	5,98	29	15,34	40	10,72
No answer	6	3,26	3	1,59	9	2,41
Altogether	184	100,00	189	100,00	373	100,00

Over 28% of respondents who think that the student council is not necessary at school[6] justify their opinion in a way that can be interpreted in correlation with mentioned earlier subjective point of view on the student council's activity ('All in all they do nothing').

16,6% of the respondents provide the objective analysis ('it would be the same without it because these are the teachers who decide')[7].

Over 8% of the respondents questioned the necessity for the student council to exist. However the reasons for giving such answers cannot be precisely explained due to the conciseness of the statements[8].

A student council's role is to organize...
discos, excursions and social events

Another issue that can be analyzed on the basis of collected empirical material is what I would call 'a narrow specialization' or narrow scope of functions bestowed upon a student council.

---

[6] It refers to answers *rather not, no.*
[7] It needs to be emphasized that 35% of those who responded In a negative way for the second question In the table did not provide any explanation.
[8] The most frequent responses were: *no-no, what for?*

Organizing cultural and entertaining events with the main focus placed on the latter turns out to be an essential function of the student council (Table 3).

Table 3. Functions of the student council proposed by those respondents
     who claimed to have some knowledge about it[9]

Functions of the Student Council[10]						
Responses	Girls		Boys		Altogether	
	no.	%	no.	%	no.	%
Organization of discos and social events	89	66,92	44	45,36	133	57,83
Organization of excursions	19	14,29	7	7,22	26	11,30
Organization of contests and competitions	19	14,29	5	5,15	24	10,43
Making decisions on some school matters	13	9,77	16	16,49	29	12,61
Helping other students	2	1,50	0	0,00	2	0,87
Cooperation with teachers	2	1,50	0	0,00	2	0,87

As it can be seen from the table the respondents who claimed they had some knowledge of what the student council does, the majority enumerated organizing discos, excursions and contests as the main initiatives taken. Other initiatives are pretty tame.

By contrast, there were two functions scarcely mentioned. Nonetheless, every tenth respondent enumerated specific initiatives of the student council. Unfortunately-over 6,5% of answers referred to the 'lucky number'[11]. The remainder of people – 3% – cited initiatives taken in order to satisfy the students needs, such as: desks in the hall, mirrors in toilets, school bulletin, music during a school break. However these answers are only a few compared with the number of students ready to have fun at school.

The function of a student council to provide cultural and social events at school is not only the most important function but also the basic criterion of the evaluation of it's activity. Every fourth respondent, that positively evaluates the work of the student council (143 persons), explains that the student council fulfills its duties well, frequently referring to organization of social events. This is the most frequent reason for the positive evaluation.

---

[9] Responses In the table are grouped into categories which were created as a result of a qualitative analysis. Each respondent gave no more than three answers.

[10] The percentage has been calculated from the number of respondents who for a question: 'Do you know what the student council in your school deals with?', answered: 'yes, I do' or 'I think so' (girls – 133, boys – 97, i.e. 230 in total).

[11] Lucky number-each student has got a number in a class register. Every day one number is drawn and one person from the class is relieved from being tested on that day – author's remark.

The phenomenon of 'entertaining function' of a student council being the most important for students cannot be easily explained. On the one hand it should be analyzed in the context of consumerism. The world where the young happen to live, is the world where everyday life triumphs (Melosik, 2004, p. 74), and having fun brings happiness. This does not facilitate searching satisfaction in other areas of life (and can even hinder such needs). On the other hand, this 'narrow specialization' of a student council may result from some policy of supporting or a consent on some kind of action, which manifests itself in the students awareness and knowledge of the scope of the student council's activity.

Summary

The findings of the research only outline some of the contemporary aspects of a student council work. This preliminary evidence provides some information on the existing problems. However more research is needed to make realistic diagnoses. Although some positive conclusions can be reached, the main objective of my study was to concentrate on the malfunctions of the student council.

In this respect, the following series of problems arise:
1. Lack of identification of students with a student council (THEY constitute the student council not US).
2. Lack of sense of democratic bestowal of power in relation to student council authorities.
3. Lack of sense of being represented by the student council authorities and the sense that the authorities act in students' interest.
4. Isolation, and in extreme cases elitism of student council authorities.
5. Lack of confidence in student council authorities, and even perceiving them as a hostile body which entered into an agreement with the teachers.
6. Limited scope of student council's activity.
7. Negative attitude towards student council's activity.

Qualitative analysis of the data collected proves that the majority of problems enumerated are due to the lack of democratization at school. In view of many students school still is a hierarchical institution based on superiority-inferiority relationships. Students cannot fancy there to be any person ready to listen to what they have to say (unless it is related to the classroom activities), let alone empowering them to make important decisions. Moreover, it turns out that what Julian Radziewicz and Maria Mirgos wrote in 1988 in their book entitled *O samorządności uczniów w procesie wychowania szkolnego* namely that we cannot teach self-governing by means of single formal, legislative and organizational acts (Cf. Radziewicz, Mirgos, 1988, pp. 75–76) remains to be true although it has been twenty years now since a student council stopped to be burdened with politicization of the past epoch.

It needs to be emphasized that a student council should not be managed by anyone but only supported or inspired and shaping self-governing is a process-not a result of a few decisions.

On the other hand, I believe that the problems of a student self-governing organization depicted here, can be a manifestation of various changes in a society. Young people develop the sense of their own identity in a specific context. Globalism, consumerism, Internet society, crisis of democracies, and especially the crisis of the civic society connected with scandal politics (Castells, 2008, pp. 354–363), decline of confidence in representative authorities, crisis of the credibility of a political system [seized-like Manuel Castells claims-in a media space, reduced to a personalized leadership dependent on technically sophisticated manipulation, incited by political scandals and driven towards them (*ibidem*, p. 364)] – all this provides the background of creating social identity. I believe, that on the level of students self-governing we can notice some projections of the crisis of civic society. One of the consequences can be-on the one hand-the dogmatic way of thinking about the school democracy and evaluating it, which is very much alike with opinion of adults on the credibility of the political systems ('a few students, who promise a lot, but do not fulfill any promise or only to some extent') and on the other hand resistance and negative attitude towards any forms that are perceived by students (rightly or not) as the ones that express dominance. Finally, another consequence of the projection of this crisis can be the anxiety over the democratization of school life. It may be the case that people whose role is to support or inspire the students activity are not willing to, or are unable to face the difficulties and resort to some alternative solutions which only lead to the lack of democracy. The problems discussed in this article, referring to the students self-governing in the context of contemporary upbringing will be further diagnosed and redefined in my future research.

References

Castells M., *Siła tożsamości*, przeł. S. Szymański, Warszawa 2008.
Fuks T., *Prawo człowieka do uczestniczenia w kierowaniu sprawami publicznymi. Standardy międzynarodowe i ich realizacja w Polsce*, Wrocław 1995.
Konstytucja Rzeczypospolitej Polskiej z dnia 2 kwietnia 1997 r., Dz. U. z 1997 r. Nr 78, poz. 483.
Kozioł R., *Samorząd. Istota, cechy, rodzaje* [w:] A. Jaeschke, M. Mikołajczyk (red.), *Co znaczył i znaczy samorząd*, Kraków 2000.

Melosik Z., *Kultura popularna jako czynnik socjalizacji* [w:] Z. Kwieciński, B. Śliwerski (red.), *Pedagogika*, t. 2, Warszawa 2004.

Radziewicz J., Mirgos M., *O samorządności uczniów w procesie wychowania szkolnego*, Warszawa 1988.

Ustawa o systemie oświaty z dnia 7 września 1991 r., Dz. U. z 2004 r. Nr 256, poz. 2572.

Renata	Care – upbringing – prevention
Miszczuk	on the example of the 'Brachu'
	Youth Community Centre
	in Kielce

A proceeding transformation of societies along with a sudden growth of civilization has recently been observed. The omnipresent, dynamic changes have a significant influence on the most important, basic human environment – the family. Every day each family has to meet not only new challenges and chances but also many problems. Without any doubts, at present realities the family is exposed to many threats. Such factors as: a deteriorating economic situation, unemployment, the increasing costs of living, an escalation of pathological phenomena have a negative impact on a condition of a family itself and its development. Supporting a family in such demanding times as now is extremely time-consuming. Very often busy, stressed parents neglect their protective duties towards their children. Their sustained work, an excess of responsibilities, a lot of efforts to improve their financial situation, cause that a child even though it is a part of a family very often is left alone with all its problems and worries. The family afflicted by different problems and crises needs more than ever a complex support. The support of a protective and educational function of the family is offered by many institutions but in this work I will focus on the educational, care and preventive activity directed to children and family realized by the 'Brachu' Youth Community Centre in Kielce founded by the PROREW Society.

The main tasks of the PROREW Society are:
- an assistance to people left on the margins of society including rehabilitation, readaptation, resocialization, revalidation;
- help to people who are addicted, co-addicted or threatened by addiction to psychotropic substances;
- providing care to so called 'street children', aggrieved children and young people threatened by social pathologies;
- prevention of social threats;
- activation of disabled people into social and professional life by public use activities and volunteering;

– supporting young people's abilities to organize themselves and cooperate;
– stimulation of young people to active and creative actions for their local society.

The idea of the PROREW Society arose both among the academics and students of the Faculty of Pedagogy and Art of the Świętokrzyska Academy in Kielce, especially among members of the GRYPS Academic Association. The main goal of the society is both educational and care, and preventive and therapeutic assistance to people left on the margins of society.

The PROREW Society has been operating since 21st February 2007 and is a non-governmental organization. We operate mainly in the area of Kielce (our facilities are located right there) but some of our activities are realized also in other parts of the Świętokrzyski region. We are planning a further development of our facilities both in the area of Kielce and the whole Świętokrzyski region.

We are a rather small organization which runs an educational and care facility offering a daily support to children and young people. We also run the Advisory Point 'Serce na Dłoni' where we realize the counseling.

The foundation of the 'Brachu' Youth Community Centre was proposed by members of the Association who belonged to PROREW Society, which as mentioned before gives an tremendous weight to all activities directed to so called 'street children', aggrieved children and young people threatened by social pathologies. The Youth Community Centre, which idea firstly appeared as early as in the year 2007, operates as a part of the Local Child and Family Support System (Lokalny System Pomocy Dziecku i Rodzinie) in Kielce.

The main element of the whole childcare system is the family while its other components are only some specific forms of support, supplement or replacement of the family's basic educational and care functions (Lubiński, 1997, p. 363). Both direct – family, school, and indirect educational environments like educational and care facilities and institutions have a strong influence on life conditions of children and youths

According to the Regulation of the Minister of Labour and Social Policy of 19th October 2007 on educational and care facilities there are the following types of such facilities: emergency facilities, family facilities, socializing facilities, daily support facilities and multifunctional facilities realizing tasks of all mentioned types of facilities.

Youth community centers apart from child support facilities and local children's clubs are one of the daily support facilities. Their main task is not only to provide children and young people also those socially maladjusted, who are partly or completely deprived of their own family's care with daily or round-the-clock, constant or temporary care but also supporting parents in the process of upbringing and taking care of a child (Bragiel, Badora, 2005, p. 220). The most important task of youth community centers is to help the family to prepare a child to an independent existence.

Those facilities should support the family in realizing its basic functions and provide an appropriate assistance to the family and children who cause discipline difficulties, are threatened by moral decay or have problems to adapt to the society.

In order to realize their tasks extensively, youth community centers should cooperate with schools, welfare centers and all other institutions which help to solve educational problems. A multidimensional, systematic approach towards the child and its family, constituting crucial conditions of life and development for a young person, seems to be essential to carry out the family support process correctly.

The functions of a youth community centre in a contemporary educational system are very broad. Some of them are as follows:

- protective function, means to watch over the child, its security, psycho-physical condition and broad development;
- preventive function, which puts emphasis on a prevention of all abnormalities of child's development such as somatic, psychological or social ones;
- reeducational function, which emphasizes not only abnormalities in child's development but also all actions taken to even out and correct all defects and disorders which appeared in the earlier stages of development;
- stimulating function, which puts emphasize on a child's activation and strives to stimulate its all development processes (Czarniewicz, 1965, p. 2).

Youth community centers realize a lot of tasks, according to Podlaski some of them include: to provide children with care during the hours established and approved by parents, to accustom children to an independent mental work, to organize teamwork and rational rest, to stimulate a broad development, to create children's interests, to develop their gifts and talents, to cooperate systematically with parents and help them to take care of children (Podlaski, 1972, p. 22).

In today's fast changing and dynamic world youth community centers with their preventive and therapeutic function are of a great importance. Their preventive activities may include providing children and youths with so valuable to them information backup, many positive experiences, possibility to feel good and to increase their self-esteem but also quick and early reaction towards children and youths from so called high-risk groups that means individuals from pathological, dysfunctional and inneficient families. Therapeutic process realized by youth community centers makes young people able to overcome their own difficulties of a different kind (Brągiel, Badora, 2005). That means, it increases their self-confidence and emphasizes all reserves of an individual.

In the Local Child and Family Support System the 'Brachu' Youth Community Centre has found its place on the one of the housing estates in Kielce.

One of the main and most important objectives of the 'Brachu' Youth Community Centre is to effectively organize free time of children who stay there.

Children's free time is undoubtedly a very important sphere of pedagogical influences both for the family, school and all non-school facilities.

To make those influences really effective a few conditions must be met. The most important are the following ones:

– from the educational point of view it must be acknowledged that organizing free time activities for children and youths is as much important as the educational role of school;

– all actual needs of particular groups of children and youths must be recognized, forms and methods of a didactic work must be adjusted to those needs and forms and methods must be constantly updated;

– development of young people's independence that means that ways of spending their free time are not only organized by adults but young people gain the ability to organize their time by their own;

– more preferable are active and creative ways of spending free time, e.g. tourism.

The tutor (organizer of free time activities) of course plays the crucial role in realizing of all those assumptions (Przesławski, 1997, p. 76).

Pupils of the 'Brachu' Youth Community Centre have the possibility to realize themselves in a few interesting sections:

– 'The world of tastes and smells' – during those classes we create the 'Little Cooks' Corner' where children participate in different activities connected with cooking and broaden their knowledge about regional dishes. They prepare various delicacies such as toasts, salads, sandwiches, chips, desserts: fruit jelly, waffles with whipped cream. Thanks to the pupils' involvement during such events as: St. Andrew's Eve, birthday parties or Christmas Eve guests can always try some delicious snacks.

– 'Beauty has many faces' – those classes are directed mainly to girls but boys are also welcomed. Their main task is to familiarize young people with the subject of beauty including not only elements of visage, fashion and body care but also some practical skills connected with body shaping. We prepare fashion shows presenting fashion trends of different epochs.

– 'I dance, visit, enjoy myself' – sports and tourism classes which main aim is the development of physical condition, visiting new places and promotion of a healthy lifestyle and active ways of spending free time. They include team games (football, volleyball, basketball, badminton), meetings at the sports hall and participation in different sporting events. In the centre one can play table tennis, foosball and mini snooker.

– 'The world of colors' – during those classes children and youths acquaint themselves with new arts techniques. They improve their skills, develop imagination and manual dexterity. They paint, draw, cut, paste, tear, glue models and prepare decorations for a theatre and cabaret section.

– 'Virtual adventure' – during those classes young people familiarize themselves with Polish and world cinematography. Young film lovers prefer cartoons, adventure films and comedies which they sometimes watch in the cinema. This section gives also the opportunity to develop computer skills and acquaint oneself with Internet.

– 'Theatre and cabaret section' – helps pupils develop their acting skills. Classes are concentrated on preparations to performances and skits. After the subject of a play or a skit is chosen we all together join forces and start to train voices, skills and prepare scenery and costumes.

The art and artistic exhibitions, sports competitions, school festivities, visits to the cinema, theatre, museum, circus are only a part of the evidence that children and youths can spend their free time in a positive and creative way.

The centre also realizes different types of educational, care or preventive programs:

1. Leave yourself some time to do something great – the main aim of this programme was to organize children and youths' free time as the alternative to the use of psychotropic substances.
2. Winter holidays in the city – the aim of this project was to organize various ways of spending free time in winter in connection with a preventive programme.
3. The world without frontiers – The world without aid substances – the purpose of this project was to conduct workshops preventing drug addiction.
4. My future – New perspectives – the idea of this course was to give equal opportunities to all young people, especially from dysfunctional families, entering the world of adults by inspiring them to being more enterprising, creative and able to plan their future.
5. What you can find in a book, you can find in your soul – the purpose of this project was to prevent social pathologies by organizing integration and preventive meetings among housing estate communities to increase their level of cultural development by promoting art and literature.
6. A good cure for one habit is another one – the aim of this project was to realize programs and workshops preventing all kinds of addiction in the area of Kielce: in the youth community centers.
7. Activity as a key to the future – a preventive programme which main goal was to take care of children and their families.
8. Life is like a theatre – the choice of a part depends on you – the idea of the project was to organize drama workshops for children and young people (workshops, performances, drama lessons, meetings with actors).
9. The art of model-making is handed down from generation to generation – the aim of this project was to organize model-making classes – workshops, displays.
10. Following the tracks of Świetokrzyski region legends – the purpose of this project was to organize sightseeing trips connected with preventive workshops as the alternative way of spending free time to the use of psychotropic substances.

At school and adolescent age children significantly develop and enrich their forms of activity. Young people involve in many complex social relations, undergo various influences (intended or unintended) and they organize their activities more or less deliberately. Their most typical and dominating form of activity is school learning and social activity in their peer groups. During the didactic process conducted in the youth community centre pupils are not only provided with some store of information and they have some abilities and habits formed but they also develop socially approved moral conducts, new incentives to act and new interests. Some situations are created intentionally to give children and youths possibilities to develop their own different forms of activity, to organize their own experiences (Sobońska, 1997, p. 24).

The project of the 'Brachu' Youth Community Centre has been created for young people and their families. Its main idea is to help children and youths from different wychowawczy societies, especially form dysfunctional, pathological and inneficient families. Present reality makes families face many problems and threats. The family as a basic social cell, to function properly and optimally, should have the possibility to obtain support in all difficult stages of its existence, from various organizations and institutions. Such support is offered by the 'Brachu' Youth Community Centre. This facility meets needs of the modern family and helps to realize its essential functions and tasks.

References

Brągiel J., Badora S. (red.), *Formy opieki, wychowania i wsparcia w zreformowanym systemie pomocy społecznej*, Opole 2005.

Czapów C., *Opieka nad dzieckiem* [w:] W. Pomykało (red.), *Encyklopedia pedagogiczna*, Warszawa 1997.

Czarniewicz M., *Funkcja placówki pozaszkolnej w systemie oświaty i wychowania*, „Biuletyn Pedagogiczny" Pałacu Młodzieży w Warszawie 1965, 4(23), 2.

Lubiński G., *Metodyka pracy opiekuńczo-wychowawczej* [w:] W. Pomykało (red.), *Encyklopedia pedagogiczna*, Warszawa 1997.

Muszyński H., *Teoretyczne problemy wychowania moralnego*, Warszawa 1965.

Podlaski J., *Formy i metody pracy świetlicowej*, Warszawa 1972.

Przesławski K., *Czas wolny dzieci i młodzieży* [w:] W. Pomykało (red.), *Encyklopedia pedagogiczna*, Warszawa 1997.

Sobońska J., *Aktywność psychomotoryczna dzieci i młodzieży* [w:] W. Pomykało (red.), *Encyklopedia pedagogiczna*, Warszawa 1997.

Stojanowska W., *Rozwód a dobro dziecka*, Warszawa 1979.

Grażyna
Durka

Phenomenon of smoking cigarettes among teenagers

Introduction

Tobacco smoking has been – for many years – the main factor threatening the health of population all over the world, including Poland. Tobacco smoking is one of the most common anti-health elements of lifestyle.

Nicotine found in cigarettes is a very powerful poison, the small quantities of which stimulate the functions of system, while the larger quantities lead to poisonings and death as the result of the respiratory centre paralysis. It has been conclusively proven that smoking is connected with the lung and bronchial cancer, as well as other chronic diseases. Hence, the habitual cigarette smoking is referred to as 'nicotinism'. Nicotine is becoming a lifestyle and a mechanical impulse for a considerable number of people.

The harmfulness of cigarette smoking is being hotly debated at present, however, few people realise how many serious diseases are connected with this addiction. The addiction to nicotine is as strong as the addiction to drugs or alcohol. This habit in the course of time has become common and only teenagers and children treat cigarette smoking as something prestigious. The addiction of smoking should be perceived as a medical problem, and, as it happens with medical diseases, treated like any other sickness afflicting a common person.

The habit of tobacco-smoking has been known for many centuries. The native Americans, even before their continent was discovered by Christopher Columbus, had smoked, chewed and inhaled tabac. The word 'tabac' originated from 'Tabasco', a place in Mexico. There, this plant was grown by Indians and it is where it was taken to Europe from in 1519.

The first information on tobacco and its seeds was brought to Europe by Romano Pane, a member of a Columbus expedition.

The word 'nicotine' originated from the surname of Jean Nicot, a physician from France who fulfilled the function of an ambassador in Portugal. The physician made a practice of using tobacco in the treatment of migraines and it was him who ordered its growing. When the queen Catherine de Medici found for herself the effectiveness of tobacco, under the influence of Jean Nicot she disseminated the plant. Since that time tobacco has become popular all over Europe (Gaś, 1993, p. 12).

Tobacco was brought to Europe from America in 1493. In the following decades it was grown on a continuously larger scale in various countries and it gradually found consumers, even though its form was completely different from the one produced today – cigarettes weren't manufactured back then, tobacco was used in the form of snuff (Piotrowski, Lisiewicz, 1983, p. 7). In 1650 a Polish representative in Turkey, Paweł Uchański, brought tobacco to Poland. The word 'tytoń' (Polish name for tobacco) originated from the Ottoman-Turkish language word of 'tiutiun' which means 'smoke'.

In the years of 1960–1980 there was a huge development of scientific research concerning the effects of smoking tobacco. It was reflected in the publishing many thousands of scientific research works. In 1964 there were about 6000 articles concerning this problem, and in 1979 there was a record of publications exceeding the number of 30 000 on various aspects of harmfulness of tobacco smoking. In this period for the first time the attention was drawn to the harmful effects of smoking tobacco on the process of pregnancy and on the foetus. In addition, it was proven that children born to smoking mothers show a number of deviations in comparison with children born to non-smoking mothers (*ibidem*, p. 8).

In spite of clear evidence concerning the harmfulness of nicotine, the phenomenon of smoking is spreading in many countries.

More and more young people take up smoking; it is considered good taste. Children smoke in younger and younger ages, which is perceived as the reason to feel proud and show-off; they smoke to feel adult, out of the need to be noticed and accepted by the smoking peers.

Young people display the feeling of being lost in the world, look for the meaning of life, and the values they could accept as their own. They go through internal conflicts. The experiences like those are common among all young people, but not all of them are able to go through them in a constructive way.

Tobacco smoking in Poland is a social problem of huge proportions. It is the most important cause of premature mortality in our country. Each year 100 thousand of deaths in Poland have a direct relation with negative effects of tobacco smoking.

In Poland until not long ago, 12 million used to smoke, including 60% of grown-up men and 30 % of grown-up women. At present over 9 million smoke. In the population of adults, over a half smoke. An average Pole smokes about 2500–3000 cigarettes annually. As early as 1976, a Pole smoked 2970 cigarettes, which back then placed him ahead of all nations in the world. Tobacco smoking currently kills more people than drugs, AIDS, alcohol and road accidents altogether. One fourth of the fires is caused by smokers. In the Wrocław Province itself, there were about 1000 fires annually. Those facts manifest a serious threat to health and lives of Poles, and especially to children, teenagers and women (Cekiera, 2001, p. 12).

Tobacco smoking causes many diseases and disorders in the development of man, and especially young man, on whom as a rule the closest peer environment has an influence.

Nicotine is the cause of cancer illnesses, circulatory and respiratory systems illnesses, and especially of the nervous system illnesses. In case of young smokers characteristic symptoms can be noticed in a form of deterioration of the senses of smell, hearing, taste and sight. Most likely, in a longer perspective smoking has an influence on personality traits. Young smokers are more often subject to emotional and neurotic (timidity, insomnia) disorders which lead to negative consequences in the form of bad studying results; the sense of anxiety and impulsiveness is also caused.

The mechanism of smoking among the youth at junior-high schools is connected with the need to demonstrate adulthood which often takes pathological forms (nicotinism, drunkenness, drug addiction). This phenomenon takes a particularly glaring form in the case of individuals with disturbed self-esteem, strangers to the process of growing up and appropriate manifestations of social maturity. Another motive is the imitation of peers from the class, or the adaptation to smokers with the aim of gaining their acceptance, and simultaneously – adding self-confidence.

The phenomenon of tobacco smoking among teenagers has a group nature. Most often, it is not a nicotine addiction, but results from the preferred and accepted life-style of a certain group of teenagers. The lack of practised alternative ways of spending time, the need to be an accepted part of a peer group results in a commonly seen teenage life-style connected with cigarette smoking and other pathologies. The functioning of such groups of teenagers is most often connected with the following characteristics:

- the disrupting of the process of care and bringing up (lack of supervision, failure to teach the teenagers other pastime forms, permanently busy parents);
- a strong need of affiliation and acceptance which has not been satisfied in a sufficient degree by the family;
- social and individual attitudes have not been fully formed, which results in disorders of the need to develop mentally and physically, and the manifestation of passive attitudes.

An important factor in the problem of smoking by school teenagers is the fashion to smoke, and the relation of society to the phenomenon of smoking, which is excessively tolerant. Preventive talks do not convince the teenagers, they are convinced by the example of common smoking among adults, and especially by the groups which serve as role-models for the teenagers: parents, teachers, doctors. The smoking by the parents has a particularly negative influence, because:

- it increases the likelihood of the occurrence of diseases among smoking parents;
- it is conducive for the occurrence of health disorders among children (passive smokers);
- it is one of the most important factors behind the early taking up of smoking by children.

The most frequent reason for taking up smoking among children, teenagers, as well as adults is the influence of the others. Most commonly, it is the influence of the peers, school colleagues, family members, acquaintances from work or the army. An important factor is also the desire to prove one's adulthood, to impress the others or just a sheer curiosity. It also happens that the first contact with cigarettes takes place in a stressful situation (Cekiera, 2001, p. 63).

An addiction made a habit at the teenage stage, in most cases persistently bothers all life long. Man, despite the fact that he has the knowledge of harmfulness of tobacco smoking, treats all those diseases with incredulity.

In the case of smoking, it is treated as a sign of protest against the limitation of freedom by parents, and the right to decide about one's life. Frequently, it is a desire to conform to the currently prevailing style in a given environment. One of the main causes of addictions is the emotional immaturity, personality disorders, a serious stress and traumas, which considerably violate the mental equilibrium. The risk of falling into addiction is increased by a negative pressure of the environment in which one functions, for example, a peer group; a young man finds it extremely difficult to say no to the remaining group members, because he or she is afraid of losing in it a position which is important to him or her.

The smoking students consider themselves to be more mature, self-reliant and grown-up in comparison with the non-smoking ones. Smoking is like an attribute of authority and maturity, it serves as a way of improving one's self-esteem, a way of dealing with stress and failures. The other cause of taking up cigarettes by the teenagers is genetic conditioning, however, no disorders have been found in the organism, which would force a given person to take up smoking, which is why the psyche is the sphere responsible for additions. One could add, that the phenomenon of cigarette-addiction is connected with an adolescent phase of life, when the psyche is not stabilized yet, and the personality not developed. Through smoking, young people try to draw attention to themselves, their troubles and problems. At this stage it is not about the pleasure of smoking, but about dealing with one's insecurity. Hence, initially, cigarette smoking serves the purpose of the young man to affirm his or her ego and artificially constructed image of a grown-up man. Such a person and his or her activities change, the younger he or she is, the more rapid the changes.

Teenagers try to adjust to new external requirements the results of which are social interactions as well as the requirements which are purposefully set in the process of educational influence. If a young man fails to meet those requirements and feels inferior to his peers, he starts looking for an alternative way – usually he takes up smoking. Then, he has the impression that his self-esteem improves and nothing could be further from the truth (Kozłowski, 1996).

Taking up smoking by teenagers is highly dangerous, because the moment of biological addiction and simple custom come imperceptibly. The process of smoking at an early stage will sooner or later take its toll on the general health of the organism. The influence of toxic substances starts in the respiratory system. Blood circulation system is also exposed to danger. Nicotine quickens one's heart-rate and raises arterial pressure of a young person. At a further stage smoking leads to arteriosclerosis.

On the basis of statistical data, in the course of 2007 in Poland there were 28,2% of smokers. The number of smoking students increases proportionally with age. In a primary school during the past year 2,6% of the polled 13 year-old students admitted to smoking, while in a junior-high school this number increases almost ten-fold – 26%, and in the post-secondary schools almost by 15-fold – 38%. What is alarming, the most considerable number is constituted by individuals smoking on a daily basis – in a junior-high school 9,5% and in a post-secondary school 11,4%.

Such a tendency in Poland is confirmed by data concerning smoking in the last month before the poll was taken: The largest group consists of people who smoked 10 times or more during the week – 9,8% in a junior-high school, and 13,8% in a post-secondary school. Those results are lower in comparison with the average poll results for Poland. Just to give an example from those average results of KBPN from 2003: 31% of teenagers smoke on a regular basis (Markiewicz, 1999, p. 109).

Results

This alarming phenomenon resulted in a need to conduct a research among school teenagers in the Pomeranian Province. The research was conducted among teenagers of junior-high schools in 2007. For the purpose of the research a method of diagnostic survey was employed. The technique employed was a poll, and the tool – a poll questionnaire. 60 people participated in the research, including 55% women and 45% men. The subject of the research was the state of knowledge on the part of students in relation to the phenomenon of smoking cigarettes. The answers sought after were the scale of the phenomenon, its causes and teenagers' attitude to smoking people. Out of the polled students 8% admitted to smoking.

Basing on their own observations and on heard stories, the polled students indicated that the most common cause of smoking among students is 'fun' (31%) and the desire to impress the peers (24%) as well as the imitation – 'because others do it, too' (16%). Both women and men gave the same answer.

A very important element in the nicotine initiation is the ability to say no in cases when the peer group tries to persuade a student to smoke 'the first cigarette'.

Unfortunately, the pressure of the peer group is so strong that not everybody can resist it. 30% of the polled students were being persuaded to smoke, 20% resisted, and 50% of the polled students were never persuaded to smoke.

The most common arguments persuading to smoke were:
– 'don't be a loser' – 30%,
– 'don't be a child' – 25%,
– 'others do it, too' – 20%,
– 'see how pleasant it is' – 10%,
– 'nothing bad is going to happen to you' – 10%,
– 'nobody is going to know' – 5%.

Among the polled students not everybody was able to resist the peer pressure. The arguments were so strong and convincing that they yielded to the persuasion and tried their first cigarette in life. 10% of the polled students yielded to this persuasion.

And here is how they motivated their decision to smoke their first cigarette:
– the fear they would be made fun of by their peers – 30%,
– the fear they might be persecuted – 15%,
– the fear they might be rejected by the group – 10%,
– the fear that they might feel inferior and humiliated – 5%.

The polled students gave their answers concerning the question where they have their 'cigarette money' from.

The most common answers were:
– pocket money – 40%,
– occasional money from family – 30%,
– rewards for petty works – 20%.

The polled were also asked where their peers get their 'cigarette money'. On the basis of their own observations and heard stories, they enumerated: pocket money – 50%, money stolen from their parents – 15% and occasional money given by their families – 5%.

The place in which nicotine initiation happens most commonly is a suburban park (60%), a school pitch (50%), a party or an excursion (30%). Those are the places where teenagers feel safest and without any supervision on the part of their parents or teachers. More seldom they smoke in their houses or school toilets (5%).

The polled teenagers have a good knowledge of the scale of smoking among their peers. On the basis of this knowledge one can conclude that the phenomenon of smoking among students does not reach excessively high levels and fluctuates between 10% and 20% of the student community.

The attitude of non-smoking peers to the smoking ones is rather indifferent (50%) or negative (20%). 10% of the non-smoking students have a positive attitude. In a similar fashion, the attitude of the smoking students to the non-smoking ones is as follows: 49% are indifferent, 30% see them in positive light, and 19% of them treat the non-smokers negatively.

The indifferent or negative attitude to the smoking people may result from the fact that schools organise preventive classes concerning the harmfulness of smoking. Most often, those classes were conducted in the form of talks (40%), discussions (30%), or watching movies on the effects and mechanisms of addictions (20%). The students' consciousness of the harmfulness of smoking is high and constitutes as much as 70% of the polled people.

What is surprising is the fact that having such considerable information on the harmfulness of cigarette smoking, 77% of the polled teenagers are in favour of the legal selling of cigarettes to minors.

The polled teenagers showed a good knowledge of cigarette brands. Brands were enumerated in the following order of popularity:
 – L&M – 35% of the polled students,
 – Viceroy – 32%,
 – Red and White – 13%,
 – Marlboro – 12%,
 – Camel – 8%.

Students were also asked whether it is easy to quit smoking. According to the polled students, 57% of them believe that it is not easy to quit it. 14% are of an opposite opinion. Among the students who used to smoke – 18% tried to quit for good, and only a small number of them did not succeed.

Out of the polled students 20% stated that they came across the phenomenon of smoking as early as in a primary school, and 25% of them – in a junior-high school. The remaining number of students did not give an answer to that question.

From this research it follows that both boys and girls smoke occasionally. It usually happens outside of school days. Boys, however, tend to smoke much more often (even a few times a week) and constitute 8% of the polled students.

Conclusion

On the basis of the conducted research, the following conclusions can be drawn:
  1. The polled teenagers had a direct contact with cigarette smoking. 8% of the polled students admitted to nicotine initiation.

2. The main reason for taking up smoking is the peer pressure. Teenagers are unable to resist it effectively, for the fear of being made fun of by their colleagues.
3. The places of cigarette smoking are those where teenagers are not supervised by their parents and teachers (park, excursion).
4. The cigarette money comes mainly from the pocket money.
5. Students attitude to smoking people is rather indifferent or negative.
6. Students show a good knowledge of cigarette brands. They were able to enumerate those brands.

Limiting the scope of the smoking phenomenon has become a priority in health programs of international health organisations and national pro-health programs. Health education at school aimed at the prevention of tobacco smoking conducted at an age when the risk of falling into addiction is particularly high, can result in the growth in the number of people who never smoke tobacco, as well as postponing in time of the decision to take up smoking, which reduces the risk of occurrence of tobacco-oriented afflictions. The experiences conducted so far it is evident that wide and constant pro-health education conducted among children and teenagers in the period of their personality development – its social and mental elements, including the biopositive habits and activities produces the best results (Polus-Szaniawska, 1996).

The prevention of cigarette-smoking among children needs to take place both at home and at school. School organises many activities with the character of primary prevention, even though they are not called in this manner, not classified in a separate program. All the actions undertaken in order to counteract pathologies, eliminate destructive effects of immature decisions and actions, to reinforce positive factors promoting acceptable attitudes are the actions aimed at preventing problems of children and teenagers.

The preventive actions should be undertaken before dangerous phenomena manifest or spread themselves. The essence of the prevention is to counteract the threats the occurrence or intensification of which in the future is highly likely.

The common opinion is that an efficient prevention is an optimal way of counteracting pathological phenomena as it is far more cost-effective than reconciliation or treatment.

Of a particular importance are educational programs which should take into consideration conditioning of tobacco smoking, its early health consequences and methods to refuse. Students must realise that their decisions to take up smoking are often made under the influence of peers, smoking parents (imitation) and advertisements. Children should have access to information on early consequences of smoking – health-oriented and cosmetic, for example: cough, coughing up of a secretion, teeth decolouration. Overcoming the addiction is possible because a young smoker has no contact with unpleasant symptoms of nicotine-hunger typical for older smokers. As long as people use and overuse nicotine, there are actions which aim at limiting its usage, and particularly by adolescents, who sometimes happen to smoke compulsively from an early stage of life (Zajączkowski, 2001).

The presented results of the research indicate the need to start a discussion on looking for more effective forms of activities to prevent tobacco smoking among teenagers. In Poland those activities are mainly limited to educational programs only used by some schools. Many years of experiences of a large number of countries indicate their low level of effectiveness. Instead, what is recommended is the mental-social approach, with the taking into account of actions in local communities, campaigns in the means of social communication and including the preventive programs into health education in schools.

References

Cekiera C., *Palenie tytoniu. Wolność czy zniewolenie?*, Lublin 2001.
Cekiera C., Zatoński W., *Palenie tytoniu*, Warszawa 2001.
Gaś Z., *Profilaktyka uzależnień*, Warszawa 1993.
Kozłowski W., *Samotność okresu dorastania*, „Nowa Szkoła" 1996, 7.
Markiewicz K., *Papierosy a zdrowie*, Warszawa 1999.
Piotrkowski J., Lisiewicz J., *Palenie tytoniu – matka – ciąża – dziecko*, „Nauka dla wszystkich" 1983, 369.
Polus-Szaniawska E., Supranowicz P., *Skuteczność działań oświatowo-zdrowotnych a palenie papierosów*, „Lider" 1996, 12.
Zajączkowski K., *Nikotyna, alkohol, narkotyki: profilaktyka uzależnień*, Kraków 2001.

Agnieszka
Próchniak

Students' attitude
to the phenomenon of cheating

Introduction

The process of teaching is connected with a great number of questions of the ethical nature. It concerns both students' behaviour and this of teachers. However, in the case of the first and the second group, improper behaviour happens – more or less consciously. In the case of teachers it can be common coming late to the classes, purposeful shortening of the classes, devoting the time of the lectures to irrelevant information, not up-dating the lectures, using swearing, organising easy final tests or exams in order to limit the number of people who take an exam once again, ignoring the phenomenon of cheating among students, ignoring unethical behaviour of other lecturers, making fun of a student in his/her presence, disclosing confidential information acquired from students to the work colleagues, omitting relevant information while writing a letter of recommendation for a student etc. (Morgan, Korschgen, 2001; Keith--Spiegel, Tabachnick, Allen, 1993).

Unfair behaviour on the part of lecturers, however, can easily be corrected by applying various sanctions such as admonitions, reprimands in writing, or dismissing a worker with a wrong attitude.

The problem of fighting with unethical behaviour on the part of students is of a different nature. At present, at universities different kinds of abuses can be encountered on the part of the studying persons. Most often, they concern false justifications for absences, cheating during exams or final tests, and the lack of the proper way of indicating the bibliography while writing theses. Using the Internet, students download virtually all theses or their parts from the Internet and act as if they are the authors. Sporadically, one can come across the cases of stealing by the students of copies of examination tests, substituting better-prepared colleagues for them at the exam in a difficult subject, or the plagiarisms of B.A. and M.A. theses. (Kennedy and others, 2000; Rakovsky, Levy, 2007).

In Poland so far many universities have started to fight against only plagiarisms of B.A. and M.A. theses. For this purpose, in some places they use a special program which allows to compare contents of a thesis with the Internet resources and evaluate to what degree this content corresponds to the one found in the Internet. In other universities this fight is merely based on the submitted, signed declarations by students that they used all the available sources in the process of preparation, and the thesis was written independently. As we can see, in relation to other ethical violations on the part of students, most universities do not state in detail any separate institutional regulations, leaving their settlement in the hands of teachers.

One of the most common offences on the part of students is cheating. Scientists have identified a number of demographic and situational factors (interactions: teacher-student, student-student, the style of conducting final tests) or psychological predispositions (educational attitudes such as: pleasure of learning, accepting the competition, believing in one's talents, the desire to learn) which are conducive to cheating.

In the researches of the demographic background it turns out that at universities those are rather men and not women who tend to cheat, younger students rather than the older, and those who receive a financial support from their parents (Whitley, 1998; McCabe, Trevino, 1997; Jordan, 2001, Vandehey, Diekhoff, La Beff, 2007).

Some researches indicate that a certain social context inspires unfair behaviour types. A particular role is played here by the attitudes of the teacher and other students in relation to persons who behave in an unethical way, which can suppress or even reinforce such a type of behaviour.

In the case of the teacher-student interaction, the students tend to cheat less when the teacher indicates real consequences of their unfair behaviour. However, this factor is not sufficient to prevent such actions. Mere commentaries on unethical aspects of cheating have little influence on the behaviour of students who may ignore such information (Robinson and others, 2004). What is essential here is the definite reaction on the part of the teacher in the form of giving a serious punishment. It has been made known from the researches that students caught cheating are more afraid of punishments in the form of unsatisfactory grades, being made to leave the classroom or disciplinary actions on the part of university authorities such as being expelled than the feeling of guilt, disapproval on the part of friends or disappointment with their attitude on the part of the family. (Diekhoff and others, 1996; Généreux, McLeod, 1995; Burns and others, 1998; Vandehey, Diekhoff, La Beff, 2007). If a punishment for cheating is not serious and only comes down to rebuking the student, taking away his crib or lowering their grade by half a mark, it does not effectively deter anybody away from cheating.

Situations when a teacher leaves a classroom during an exam or reads a newspaper not paying any attention to students' behaviour also undoubtedly reinforce unethical actions on the part of students and considerably reduce a level of knowledge 'acquired' in such a way. The organization of an exam for large groups of students, whom the teacher in charge is unable to supervise, using the same test questions or the whole question sets can also lead to abuses. Allowing students to use their own sheets of paper or the whole note-books, without previously checking them for prepared copies of an exam is creating the environment conducive to cheating.

Students cheat less when they perceive their teachers as matter-of-fact people who emphasise the intrinsic values of studying, treat them with respect and understanding, and when they notice that those teachers do not prepare overly difficult tests for unjustified reasons. The willingness to cheat, however, rises when, in their perception, the classes are boring, trivial in content or irrelevant, and they regard the teachers as people who are insensitive, unfriendly and in a bad mood. (Généreux, McLeod, 1995; Diekhoff and others, 1996; McCabe, Trevino, 1997; Robinson and others, 2004).

In the case of the student-student interaction, the willingness to cheat manifests itself among those students who are convinced that cheating is a common phenomenon during studying, as well as among their peers in a group. It can also be reinforced among those of them who can directly observe their colleagues who cheat and benefit from it. There are researches which indicate that students can cheat when they believe that their peers tolerate such behaviour and when they live with people who behave in a similar fashion. (Diekhoff and others, 1996; McCabe, Trevino, 1997; Jordan, 2001; Robinson and others, 2004).

Students who emphasise the understanding of the classes' content tend to cheat less than those who only want to get a good grade or simply to get a credit. In a similar fashion, those who participate in specific classes with the aim to get a good job or impress the future employer, tend to manifest a larger inclination towards unfair actions. (Davis, Ludvigson, 1995; Jordan, 2001). It also turns out that the lower grade average at the studies the student has, the higher the likelihood he/she can resort to unfair forms of getting credits (Vandehey and others, 2007). Also, those who tend to doubt their intelligence or expect they might fail an exam may be more willing to cheat at a final test. In addition, researches indicate that people inclined to cheat are among those students who are afraid they might not be up to the knowledge standards required by teachers (Davis, Ludvigson, 1995).

Cheating occurs within the limits of expected costs and losses. From the rational choice it follows that the perceived severe punishments reduce the likelihood of cheating. A large number of researches prove that the fear of the possibility of getting caught while cheating and the fear of external sanctions are the most important factor in reducing the tendency to cheat. It is, however, difficult to perceive it as the only factor which could be conducive to reducing the number of cheating students. At present it is estimated that an effective method of fighting against this phenomenon can turn out to be an effectively communicated and applied politics of educational authorities in relation to students who commit unfair actions as well as the growth of consciousness on the part of students that it is impossible to avoid punishments for unethical actions. This is why at a large number of American universities the so-called honour codes are introduced, which specify the rules of ethical behaviour at the studies – the rules that each and every student is bound to know and respect. The introduction of honour codes does not eliminate completely unethical actions on the part of students. However, researches indicate that at the places where they had been introduced and are in operation, noted unfair actions are down by approximately 25%–50%. In addiction, a person caught cheating receives a special grade of XF and cannot count on any form of financial support from the university, and, moreover, is prohibited to represent their university outside (contests, competitions) and has a ban to sit on any student organisations. (McCabe, Trevino, Butterfield, 1999; Scanlan, 2006). As we can see, a cheating person does not deserve the trust of academic community and the honour of representing its interests.

Students are conscious of the consequences of various unethical actions observed among their colleagues and the obligation to bear proper responsibilities. In one of researches, the students were asked to point out those forms of punishment they considered the most appropriate for a person caught cheating. It turned out that among the sanctions accepted by the subjects of the research were: a conversation after a class with a person caught cheating, lowering his or her test grade, offering him or her a possibility to take a test once again, or no reaction whatsoever (Carter, Punyanunt-Carter, 2006). What is interesting, in the research by Davis, the most popular form of 'punishment' in the students' perception was merely drawing the students' attention by the teacher to mind their own tests. (Davis and other, 1992). Those conclusions only indicate that students do not accept more severe consequences of their unethical actions. The preferred forms of punishment do not effectively discourage from cheating and are on the margins of losses acceptable to bear in the situation of being caught cheating.

It turns out, however, that a large number of problems concerning forms of punishments aimed at cheating students is a problem to the teachers themselves. As much as 71% of the polled teachers admitted that a confrontation with a cheating student is one of the most negative aspects of being a teacher (Keith-Spiegel and others, 1998). McCabe (1993) observes that students perceive the teachers' reaction in relation to cheating students as 'lenient'. In the research of Graham only 9% of lecturers out of 79% who caught students cheating, employed some forms of punishment in relation to them. (Graham and others, 1994). Among the reasons for the lack of an appropriate reaction in relation to cheating students, the lecturers usually give: emotional consequences (stress, career-oriented fear), lack of courage, excessive effort and time necessary to collect evidence against a person behaving in an unfair manner, failure to admit that student may cheat during his/her own classes; lack of activity and support on the part of the administrative body in reducing the level of unfair actions among students; the belief that any form of punishment is satisfactory; the fear of a potential engagement in costly court proceedings (Keith-Spiegel and others, 1998; McCabe, 1993; Volpe, Davidson, Bell, 2008). However, it turns out that the students consider it important that their lecturers unambiguously stated their preferences concerning unfair actions. In their opinion the lecturers should help the students realise why cheating is an action they should deem counter-productive and immoral.

As it can be seen, the research concerning cheating indicate that it is a phenomenon of a complex nature and subjected to many variables. A review of the researches concerning cheating allows us to form our own research hypotheses regarding the analysed phenomenon.

For the needs of my own research I assume that the polled persons treat cheating as an unfair form of getting credits and it is a commonly occurring phenomenon at the studies. I also assume that for the polled people its is a risky form of getting credits and better grades, which cannot be eliminated even by the way of severe forms of punishment in relation to cheating students.

I further assume that the attitude of the polled people to this phenomenon is subjected to various socio-demographic variables.

Method

Characterization of the polled population

The research was conducted in February 2007 among the students of Wyższa Hanzeatycka Szkoła Zarządzania (Higher Hanseatic School of Management) in Słupsk.

In total, 196 people were polled. Among this number over two-thirds of the polled (70,91%) were women, and almost one-third (29,09%) were men.

A considerable majority of the polled people (61,72%) are not older than 24 years, every fifth polled person (22,46%) is in the age bracket of 25-35 years, and 15,82% of the polled are over 35. The polled students are for the most part inhabitants of cities (68,87%) rather than rural areas (31,13%). Almost two-fifths of the polled people (38,77%) are students of full time studies, and the remaining number (61,23%) are extramural ones. Almost one-third of them receive a scholarship (32,65%), and over two-thirds of the polled (67,35%) have no such benefits.

Procedure and the description of the research tools

The research was realised by the way of an anonymous auditory poll conducted among extramural and full time students during classes with them. In the research a poll questionnaire was used which consisted of two parts. In the first of them various opinions on the subject of cheating were included. They concerned, among the others, ethical aspects of cheating, potential motives to cheat, as well as methods to eliminate this phenomenon from studies. The second part of the poll included certificate-oriented questions referring to: the respondent's gender, age, place of residence, mode of studying and whether they are currently receiving a scholarship. For the purpose of statistical analysis of the acquired results in the survey of socio-demographic qualities the Ch^2 Pearson's test was utilized.

Results of the research

The polled students were asked to react to a dozen or so opinions concerning various aspects of the phenomenon of cheating by marking the correct answer. The chart below contains the acquired results.

Table 1. Opinions of the polled students concerning the phenomenon of cheating (data in %)

Opinions concerning cheating	Yes	No	Hard to say
Cheating by no means can be eliminated among students – it has been here forever and is here to stay	85,71	8,16	6,12
Cheating is a good way of getting a credit when there is not enough time for a good preparation to get it	77,04	12,24	10,71
It is a good way to get a better 'lucky' grade	76,02	12,75	11,12
It is a risky way to get a credit in a subject	70,40	12,24	17,34
It is an unfair way to get a better grade	60,20	23,97	15,81
It is a convenient way to get a credit in a subject without investing too much of an intellectual effort	59,18	23,97	16,83
Cheating is an unfair way of getting credits in subjects	59,18	23,97	16,83
People cheat because they see that other people practise it with benefits (getter grades, scholarships, studying without intellectual effort)	56,63	28,57	14,79
Cheating is a conscious deceiving of oneself and others – pretending that one possesses knowledge in a given subject	46,42	35,72	17,86
Cheating is a manifestation of an unfair competition among students	40,30	36,23	23,47

People cheat because they dislike excessive learning	40,30	31,64	28,06
Cheating is the only way to get a credit in a difficult subject	39,79	42,35	17,86
Cheating can only be eliminated if each and every person caught cheating is subjected to a severe form of punishment	30,10	46,94	22,96
Cheating is a normal way of getting credits while studying	30,10	45,92	23,98
People cheat, because teachers are too lenient in relation to the students caught cheating – they only give them warnings, tell them to hide cribs, or take them away themselves with no consequences – instead of giving them right away unsatisfactory grades	29,08	51,54	19,38
People cheat, because they are not afraid of a punishment in the form of an unsatisfactory grade	29,08	44,38	26,54
People cheat, because they are allowed to by teachers through insufficient supervision of students at the time of writing final tests or exams	28,07	49,48	22,45
People caught cheating are to be immediately asked to leave the classroom and given unsatisfactory grades in a given subject	25,51	52,55	21,94
Cheating is an irresponsible way of treating studies and studying process which aim to acquire and not avoid knowledge	25,00	47,44	27,56
Cheating indicates lack of character and ambition on the part of the cheating person	23,98	51,54	24,48
People cheat, because nobody has ever caught them cheating	20,40	63,27	16,33
Only unambitious people tend to cheat	14,28	68,37	17,35

Source: my own study.

Over three-fourths of the polled students (85,71%) admit that cheating by no means can be eliminated among students – it has always been here and is here to stay. Approximately a half of them (46,94%) is of the opinion that even consequently applied severe forms of punishment in relation to all the students caught cheating are not going to be of any help. A considerable majority of respondents (70,40%) do not keep it secret that is a risky form of getting a credit in a subject. Despite that fact almost half of the polled students (45,92%) do not treat this phenomenon as a normal way of getting credits in subjects at the studies. It is an opinion more common among inhabitants of rural areas rather than the city (54,10% in relation to 42,22% for $p = 0,01$), extramural students rather than full time ones (49,17% in relation to 40,79% for $p = 0,001$) and people receiving scholarships (59,38% in relation to 39,39% for $p = 0,01$).

Among opinions concerning the possible reasons behind cheating the one prevailing is above the others that it is a good way to get a credit in a subject when there is not enough time for a sufficient preparation for it (77,04%). This opinion is shared by full time students rather than extramural ones (86,84% in relation to 70,83% for $p = 0,05$). A similar group of the polled students (76,02%)

believe that cheating is a good way to get a better 'lucky' grade. What is interesting, this opinion is shared by women rather than men (81,29% in relation to 63,16% for p = 0,001), full time students rather than extramural ones (86,84% in relation to 69,17% for p = 0,01) and students receiving a scholarship (82,81% in relation to 72,73% for p = 0,06). Slightly fewer students (59,18%) indicate that it is also a convenient way to get a credit in a subject without investing too much intellectual effort. Over a half of the polled students (56,63%) state that people cheat because they observe others doing it and having benefits out of it in the form of better grades and scholarships, or just studying without investing in it too much of an intellectual effort. This opinion is shared by women rather than men (63,31% in relation to 40,35% for p = 0,01). Only two-fifths of the polled students (40,30%) is of the opinion that people use cribs, because they dislike learning too much and it is exactly what is required to prepare properly for an exam or a final test. This opinion is shared by full time students rather than extramural ones (55,26% in relation to 30,83% for p = 0,001) and students not older than 24 rather than those in the age bracket of 25–35 or older (46,28% in relation to 34,09% and 25,81% for p = 0,01).

The polled students do not, however, share the opinion that people cheat because nobody has ever caught them in the process (63,27%). Those are the results for students up to 24 years old and in the age bracket of 25–35 rather than older ones (65,29% and 63,64% in relation to 54,84% for p = 0,05). In a similar fashion, they believe that cheating is not a result of teachers' leniency in relation to the students caught cheating, who only give them warnings, tell them to hide cribs or just take them away without employing any forms of stricter sanctions. (51,54%). Those are rather men than women who disagree with this opinion (63,16% in relation to 46,76% for p = 0,05) and extramural students rather than full time ones (58,33% in relation to 40,79% for p = 0,001). In addition, the polled students do not tend to share the opinion that cheating results from insufficient supervision of students by teachers at the time of writing exams or final tests (49,48%). This opinion is common mainly among students not receiving scholarships (54,55% in relation to 39,06% for p = 0,001). Only over two-fifths of the polled students (44,38%) disagree with the opinion that people may cheat because they are not afraid of a punishment in the form of an unsatisfactory grade. Slightly fewer polled students (42,35%) do not share the opinion that cheating is the only way to get a credit in a difficult subject. It is noteworthy that only 39,79% of the polled students state to the contrary, which may go to indicate that it is in the case of difficult subjects (extensive material to cover or a specific character of target problems) those students resort to cheating while taking a final test.

The majority of the polled (60,20%) unanimously agree that cheating is an unfair way of getting a better grade, as well as an unfair way of getting credits in subjects (59,18%). The last opinion is shared mainly by respondents in the age bracket of 25–35 and older rather than those not older than 24 (70,45% and 77,42% in relation to 50,41% for p = 0,001), inhabitants of the city rather than rural areas (61,48% in relation to 54,10% for p = 0,001) and extramural students rather than full time ones (67,50% in relation to 46,05% for p = 0,0001). Over two-fifths of the respondents (46,42%) also share the opinion that cheating is a conscious deceiving of oneself and others – pretending that one possesses knowledge of a subject. This is an opinion more common among women rather than men (47,48% in relation to 43,86% for p = 0,05). Slightly fewer respondents (40,30%) also believe that cheating is a manifestation of an unfair competition among students. This is an opinion more typical for women rather than men (46,76% in relation to 24,56% for p = 0,01), extramural students rather than full time ones (49,17% in relation to 26,32% for p = 0,001) and students receiving scholarships (53,13% in relation to 34,09% for p = 0,01). It needs to be added that slightly fewer respondents state to the contrary (36,23%), which may go to indicate that this group of respondents does not see cheating as an unfair method to get better grades.

Despite critical ethical attitude in relation to the phenomenon of cheating expressed by the respondents it seems curious that almost half of them (47,44%) do not agree with the opinion that cheating is an irresponsible way of treating studies and the process of studying which aim to acquire not to avoid knowledge. It is a fact that cheating is an effect of the lack of knowledge or its unsatisfactory mastering which may inspire students' fear they may not get a credit in a subject and so they resort to cheating. What is more, over a half of the polled students (52,55%) is also against asking the person caught cheating to leave the classroom and immediately giving him or her an unsatisfactory grade in a given subject by the teacher. This opinion is shared rather by students who do not receive a scholarship (59,09% in relation to 39,06% for p = 0,01). It is apparent that what we evidence here is a lack of consequence in thinking and especially the willingness to take responsibility for actions unworthy of a student. It is obvious that such an attitude is a way of deceiving not only oneself but also other students, lecturers and the university which offers scholarships. Getting better grades through cheating than those one actually deserves, and what follows – getting a higher grade average, is in this case a form of beguilement of a scholarship which might be treated as an criminal offence. What is interesting, a considerable majority of respondents (68,37%) admit that not only unambitious students tend to cheat. It is an opinion common among people not older than 24 and in the age bracket of 25–35 rather than older (75,21% and 61,36% in relation to 51,61% for p = 0,001). This may go to indicate that students also observe this phenomenon among the people who achieve good results studying, whose high ambitions and aspirations, and possibly also a fear of failure, motivate them to employ unfair forms of help in the process of writing final tests. Possibly on account of that, a half of the respondents (51,54%) do not share the opinion that cheating reveals lack of character and ambition of the cheating individual. This opinion is common among respondents not older than 24 and in the age bracket of 25–35 rather than older (55,37% and 52,27% in relation to 35,48% for p = 0,05) and full time students rather than extramural ones (64,47% in relation to 43,33% for p = 0,001).

Conclusion

It seems that the phenomenon of cheating is impossible to eliminate from students' lives as long as students themselves shall not perceive the process of knowledge acquisition as the main goal of their endeavours and derive pleasure from the very fact of studying in the chosen major. Cheating reveals that the goal is rather to get a credit in a difficult subject, get a better grade or just save the time and effort needed to master required knowledge. This form of attitude may be further reinforced by the observation of peers who cheat successfully, especially those who are rewarded for their actions by benefits in the form of better grades, and, as a result, scholarships. Such situation, in the perception of students who prepare for exams in fair, scrupulous ways and get lower grades, may inspire a justified feeling of disappointment that a fair attitude does not bring expected results. On the other hand, unfair tactics can be far more effective, and less demanding. This state of affairs may naturally lower the morale of fair students.

A certain factor in the spreading of this phenomenon may also be attributed to the lenient attitude to the cheating students on the part of the university teachers who fail to punish them adequately. The lack of clearly articulated objection and specified severe sanctions in relation to students caught cheating results in the situation when the students pay virtually no attention to the possibility of being punished for their actions. If a form of punishment is not sufficiently severe, one can hardly be surprised that students consider it more beneficial to risk and cheat, than scrupulously prepare for exams.

It seems that only the consciousness of severe sanctions for improper behaviour and their consistent execution may effectively deter at least a part of students from unethical actions. Getting a credit in a subject or taking an exam is aimed to evaluate the mastery of knowledge and student's understanding of a given field. Getting a passing grade indicates that a student has – in various degrees – mastered this knowledge. Excessive leniency of a lecturer in relation to a cheating person is – to a certain degree – a manifestation of tolerance for the lack of knowledge on the part of a student in need of unfair aids to present the required knowledge. In addition, it results in inspiring the sense of impunity in the cheating students and can lead to allowing them to get better grades – ones they do not deserve. If, by this way, a student receives a high grade average, and what follows, a scholarship, he or she receives as a result a financial benefit not for an actual state of knowledge, but just for the cunning and deception. This is why, in the case of people cheating on a regular basis, considerably more severe forms of punishment might be recommended.

The failure to eliminate or reduce this phenomenon brings specific consequences not only for students, but for the university as a whole. This kind of strategy not only lowers the level of teaching, but reflects in a negative way on the image of an educational institution. A student with a diploma of such an institution is not taken seriously by a potential employer. Apart from that, a low level of teaching is harmful for those students who worked all the years at the studies in a fair and scrupulous way. In such a situation a high level of teaching and the teaching staff are not relevant; what counts is the 'word-of-mouth' opinion of the students of a given university on how they are taught in reality. This is how the real image of their educational institution is shaped in the eyes of their closest environment- their families, friends or just casual acquaintances and not from a good reputation of the university earned in a hard way over many years.

References

Burns S. R., Davis S. R., Hoshino T., Miller R. L., *Academic dishonesty: A delineation of cross-cultural patterns*, 'College Student Journal' 1998, 32(4), 590–596.

Carter S. L., Punyanunt-Carter N. M., *Acceptability of treatments for cheating in the college classroom*, 'Journal of Instructional Psychology' 2006, 33(3), 212–216.

Davis S. F., Grover C. A., Becker A. H., McGregor L. N., *Academic dishonesty: Prevalence, determinants, techniques, and punishments*, 'Teaching of Psychology' 1992, 19, 16–20.

Davis S., Ludvigson H., *Additional data on academic dishonesty and a proposal for remediation*, 'Teaching Psychology' 1995, 22(2), 199–222.

Diekhoff G. M, LaBeff E. E., Clark R. E., Williams L. E., Francis B., Haines V. J., *College cheating: Ten years later*, 'Research in Higher Education' 1996, 37(4), 487–502.

Généreux R. L., McLeod B. A., *Circumstances surrounding cheating: A questionnaire study of college students*, 'Research in Higher Education' 1995, 36(6), 687–704.

Graham M. A., Monday J., O'Brein K., Steffen S., *Cheating in a small college: An examination of student and faculty attitudes and behaviors*, 'Journal of College Student Development' 1994, 35, 255–260.

Jordan A. E., *College student cheating: The role of motivation, perceived norms, attitudes, and knowledge of institutional policy*, 'Ethics & Behavior' 2001, 11(5), 233–247.

Keith-Spiegel P., Tabachnick B. G., Allen M., *Ethics in academia: Students' views of professors' action*, 'Ethics & Behavior' 1993, 3, 149–162.

Keith-Spiegel P., Tabachnick B. G., Whitley B. E. Jr., Washburn J., *Why professors ignore cheating: Opinions of a national sample of psychology instructors*, 'Ethics & Behavior' 1998, 8(5), 215–227.

Kennedy K., Nowak S., Raghuraman R., Thomas J., Davis S. F., *Academic dishonesty and distance learning: Student and faculty views*, 'College Student Journal' 2000, 34(2), 309–315.

McCabe D. L., *Faculty responses to academic dishonesty: The influence of student honor code*, 'Research in Higher Education' 1993, 34(5), 647–658.

McCabe D. L., Trevino L. K., *Individual and contextual influences on academic dishonesty: A multicampus investigation*, 'Research in Higher Education' 1997, 38(3), 379–396.

McCabe D. L., Trevino L. K., Butterfield K. D., *Academic integrity in honor code and non-honor code environments: A qualitative investigation*, 'Journal of Higher Education' 1999, 70(2), 29–45.

Morgan B. L., Korschgen A. J., *The ethics of faculty behavior: Students' and professors' views*, 'College Student Journal' 2001, 35(3), 418–422.

Rakovski C. C., Levy E. L., *Academic dishonesty: Perceptions of business tudents*, 'College Student Journal' 2007, 41(2), 466–481.

Robinson E., Amburgey R., Swank E., Faulkner C., *Test cheating in a rural college: Studying the importance of individual and situational factors*, 'College Student Journal' 2004, 38(3), 380–395.

Scanlan C. L., *Strategies to promote a climate of academic integrity and minimize student cheating and plagiarism*, 'Journal of Allied Health' 2006, 35(3), 179–185.

Vandehey M. A., Diekhoff G. M., La Beff E. E., *College cheating: A twenty-year follow-up and the addition of an honor code*, 'Journal of College Student Development' 2007, 47(4), 468–480.

Volpe R., Davidson L., Bell M. C., *Faculty attitudes and behaviors concerning student cheating*, 'College Student Journal' 2008, 42(1), 164–175.

Whitley B. E., *Factors associated with cheating among college student: A review*, 'Research in Higher Education' 1998, 39(3), 235–274.

Joanna
Nawrocka

Between the social norms of caring for older persons and prejudices against them

Is this thin, grey-haired lady your energetic mum? And that bowed man? Is he your vigorous father? Yes, they are. You spent your childhood with them seeing them strong, hard-working and full of plans. One day you notice them get older. Fortunately, there is enough emotional closeness between you and them as to care for and help them. So that you do your duties being in harmony with the social norms that enable you to retain a positive self-esteem. The closeness and the social norms are important because unlike in western Europe in Poland older persons are cared for by their family members. This type of care, called famcare, is carried out at home and seems to be supported by the European Union programmes.

L. Berkovitz (1972) and Gouldner (1960) think the social norms to be the source of will to help. These are the social responsibility norm and the reciprocation norm. The first one says that the more people are dependent on you the more you look after them. As your elders are dependent on you if they suffer from being ill or disabled, you try to provide them with suitable care and help. The reciprocation norm lets people expect care and help from those were looked after by them in the past. As your parents and grandparents protected you and care for you when you were a child you give back this sort of favours when they have become weaker and helpless.

The fact that people help their relatives more often than those who do not belong to their families is explained by W. Hamilton (1964) representing the evolutionary approach. Entities prefer caring for and helping their relatives to caring for and helping strangers as they seek to retain the gene set of their kin. Individuals are even ready to expose their lives to danger while saving their relatives provided the relatives are children and adolescents. Older people can rely on their family members while wanting everyday care and favours (Burnstein, Crandell, Kitayama, 1994).

The reciprocal altruism theory was conceived by R. Trivers (1971). Helping others of our species is supposed to work efficiently because individuals are aware of being benefited if they respect and realize the attitude Today I am helping and am looking after you, one day – perhaps even tomorrow – you will help and will look after me. This position was formed by our distant ancestors: hunters and gatherers. Since then it has been shared by the modern world's inhabitants, not to mention it is strongly respected in very few hunter-gatherer communities in our times (Buss, 2001). Although the theory does not directly refer to helping and caring for older persons, it explains the general rules of helping others.

M. Clark and J. Mills (1979) differentiated between the exchange and the communal relations. The latter ones are long-lasting and refer to an individual's self that makes people feel responsible for their partner's needs and offer them help and care. Moreover, they do not expect the interaction partners to respond immediately after having been given. While being in the exchange relations people are not responsible for needs of the others, and the relations are not long-lasting and do not refer to the self. The parties exchange different goods and values with each other and watch each other not remain a favour without a response. As the relation model is formed by the means of categories connected to self the relations of the both types seem to show some psychological motives for caring for older persons. One helps their elders because they and the relations with them are seen to be a part of one's self in the communal relationships. On the other hand, older persons must have done some favours that should be given back due to the exchange relations.

According to the relational model by A. Fiske (Haslem, Fiske, 1992) the four relations are said to be found all over the world. These are the communal sharing, the authority ranking, the equality matching and the market pricing. Yet only the communal sharing and/or the authority ranking seem to explain why older persons are cared for by their families. The equality matching cannot be an explanation of caring for older persons as they are not treated as the equal ones by people under 65. The market pricing may explain institutional forms of caring for older persons. The first relational type can be characterized by an approach towards one another one for all and all for one. The parties care for each other, willingly sharing all goods. In the second relation one of the parties makes most of the decisions the others go along with that person's choices. The one in charge takes responsibility for things and the others are followers knowing they can depend on the one in charge to lead and to protect them. The third type is structured on a 50:50 basis. The parties are equal in the things they do for each other. The fourth one resembles a business relation: you get precisely how much you give. This relation ends when profits for the both parties are fulfilled.

These norms do not cover the whole list of the social norms but the rest of them are not related with the discussed problem. The norms make people ready to care for their elders but on the other hand, prejudices against older persons can form ambivalent attitudes towards the aging processes and the older persons. Not only are the individuals not being in the close relations with older persons influenced by the prejudices but also those who care for their elders are not free of the stereotypical substances. It is shown by the research presented in the next paragraphs of this article.

60 persons (30 women and 30 men) were asked to make a description of an old person and his/her daily activities and then they were asked to make a description of an old person known to them and his/her daily activities. In this case the subjects could describe their mothers or fathers, grandmothers or grandfathers or another older person provided the person stays in the relationship with a subject. The age mean of the subjects is 31.5 ranging from 23 to 62.

While characterizing the unknown older person, the subjects used phrases referring to the physical appearance (ruined by the aging processes) and to a difficult personality and behavior characteristics. It has been obtained the following percentage 45%, 30%, 23%, 2%.

45% of the subjects have written that the older person has got a wrinkled face and grey hair, is bowed, physically weak, decrepit, almost blind, almost deaf, with shaky hands and a shaky head. His/her pace is unsteady. He/she is very as thin as lath or suffers from obesity. He/she is thought to be oversensitive, pretentious, malicious, narrow-minded, difficult, querulous, embittered and ugly. Moreover, the person is seen to be childish, ruminative, grumbling, highly critical towards others, incompetent and unable to control his/her life. The subjects have also described older persons as sexually abominable.

30% of the subjects have described the older person as passive and not being interested in the world, cognition and knowledge. He/she does not want to learn new things having the ill will for new technologies and not bothering about the self-actualisation processes. He/she is also said to be bored, lonely, submissive, old-fashioned, over-religious. The person pays his/her attention only to his/her comfort and takes no notice of what other people need.

The older person is thought to be obsessively concentrated on the health spending a lot of time 'in the medical centre receptions' and being hypochondriac but careless about the hygienic standards. He/she looks back to the past and suffers from dementia (23% of the subjects).

Surprisingly, the older person is rarely characterized as a family-centered individual (2% of the subjects). Moreover, he/she has knowledge of all life aspects but experiences the existential emptiness.

While characterizing the old person being in the closer relationships with the subjects, they used phrases mainly referring to wisdom, knowledge and experience. The words and the phrases of the physical appearance were used more seldom than they were written in the characteristic of the unknown older person. It has been obtained the following percentage of the subjects: 48%, 32%, 26%, 4%.

48% – The older person is described as knowledgeable of all life aspects, as a depositor of the family tradition, a depositor of the family customs. The person cooks and bakes delicious cuisine, and cherishes grandchildren. The person is thought to be wise, careful about religious customs, full of reverence for the country and its history. He/she is believed to be tender for family members. He/she tends to forgive others irrespective of their 'sins'.

32% – The older person is perceived to respect people and to have a tender conscience. He/she is said to have unusual, spiritual experiences and to explore some life mysteries. The older person is thought to judge people adequately and to see others through. The subjects consider the elder person having an insight into the death experience and making philosophical enquiries. The person is seen to be sensible and with a good sense of humor.

26% – The subjects notice the older person be sensitive to the natural environment, emotional and lonely. The person is characterized by being oversensitive and depressive. The older person appears to be ill and to need help and care. He/she is thought to be old-fashioned, overprotective towards others. His/her face is not characterized as wrinkled but as interesting.

4% – Few subjects consider the older person a grumbler, decrepit and bowed.

There were less negative descriptions of the known older person in comparison with the first description as the stereotyping processes and the stereotypes' substances were diminished by the emotional closeness to the older person. The descriptions of the unknown older individual were concentrated on the physical aspects of an older person that can be explained by the fact that the physical features are the basis of stereotyping and prejudice against older persons (Zebrowitz, Montepare, 2002). They are noticed as ugly and decrepit, and the vivid image of aging can cause other aspects of negative stereotyping.

Health is seen to be the core of daily activities of older persons – 62% of the subjects making the descriptions of the unknown older person and 53% of the subjects making the descriptions of the known one. Irrespective of describing the unknown or the known older person the subjects characterized them by using the similar phrases. The older person is thought to be often hospitalized, is concentrated on his/her health by changing/respecting a diet and/or doing gymnastics. He/she is said to take a lot of medicines, to suffer from many diseases, to be treated permanently and to visit different physicians very often or regularly. Not accepting some changes in his/her appearance is also mentioned by the subjects but with a slight difference. While characterizing the known person the subjects spontaneously wrote about recalling of the past looks by the older person. When the subjects made the descriptions of the unknown older person, they told their reasons such as 'criticising the beauty of youngsters' and 'having cosmetic surgeries'.

Other daily activities were not connected to the health conditions and the subjects differentiated the unknown old person from the known one. The unknown person is characterized by the phrases of negative significance. He/she is believed to attract others' attention by telling about his/her diseases and to overestimate his/her illnesses. The person appears not to do anything apart from watching TV a lot, having heated arguments with family members and going on a pilgrimage that is interrupted by complaining about his/her poverty – 21% of the subjects. The known person of an age is seen in the better light – 29% of the subjects. He/she continues his/her work as a part–time job, celebrates everyday life and devotes himself/herself to hobbies and passions that could not be realized before being retired. This person does not forget to feed homeless animals a few times a day.

The subjects are aware of a peculiar type of activities that are realized by older people more often than by younger ones. Irrespective of being unknown (17%) or being known (19%) to the subjects, older people are perceived to teach youngsters how to live happily. They also discuss religious/ theological/ philosophical problems with their peers and family members as well. The older people are seen not to be afraid of death. They also understand and reveal the meanings of all experiences that are veiled for younger people. This type of activities appears to pertain to the social roles of older people who are expected to dispense their knowledge to others. This knowledge is supposed to console effectively all those unhappy and disappointed by some misfortunes.

The knowledge, resulting in psychotherapeutic effects, seems to be rooted in the philosophical concept of serenitas animi. It was conceived at the beginning of restless Roman Empire period. Since that epoch it has had enough time to be strengthened intellectually and to influence on the usual people's minds. Serenitas animi interprets being old in the terms of the time of understanding the consciousness and the universe phenomena. The deep understanding was supposed to give a lot of peace to the older persons' souls. This idealized vision of vigorous and wise old persons was used a criterion of the last stage of men's lives. (Women were not included in the concept but it does not matter much as in that stage most of them did not survive until they got older.) In the late 60s of the 20th century serenitas animi was shaken not only by the changing living and working conditions but also by some writers and philosophers (Amery, 1967/2007; Przybylski, 1998). Since then it has not regained its glorious significance.

The phrases collected in the research were perfected as for the language style becoming the basis of the following methods: The questionnaire of aging; The older people's attributes questionnaire; The attitudes towards older people scale; The attitudes towards older consumers scale. The first method includes 120 items, the second one – 149 items, the third one – 95 items and the fourth one – 80 items. The researches into the social experience of aging and the social judgments on older persons are being carried out by the means of the methods.

References

Amery J., *O starzeniu się. Podnieść na siebie rękę*, przeł. B. Baran, Warszawa 1968/2007.

Berkovitz L., *Social norms, feelings and other factors affecting helping and altruism*, 'Advances in Experimental Social Psychology' 1972, 6, 63–108.

Burnstein E., Crandell S., Kitayama S., *Some neo-Darwinian rules for altruism: Weighing cues for inclusive fitness as a function of the biological importance of the decision*, 'Journal of Personality and Social Psychology' 1994, 67, 773–789.

Buss D. M., *Psychologia ewolucyjna. Jak wytłumaczyć społeczne zachowanie człowieka. Najnowsze koncepcje*, przeł. M. Przylipiak, Gdańsk 2001.

Clark M. S., Mills J., *Interpersonal attraction in exchange and communal relationships*, 'Journal of Personality and Social Psychology' 1979, 37, 12–24.

Gouldner A. W., *The norm of reciprocity: A preliminary statement*, 'American Sociological Review' 1960, 25, 161–178.

Hamilton W. D., *The genetical evolution of social bevavior*, 'Journal of Theoretical Biology' 1964, 7, 1–16.

Haslem N., Fiske A. F., *Implicit relational prototypes: Investigating five theories of the cognitive organization of social relationships*, 'Journal of Experimental Social Psychology' 1992, 28, 441–474.

Kołodzieczyk W., *Stereotypy dotyczące starzenia się i ludzi w podeszłym wieku* [w:] S. Steuden, M. Marczuk (red.), *Starzenie się a satysfakcja z życia*, Lublin 2006.

Przybylski R., *Baśń zimowa. Esej o starości*, Warszawa 1998.

Synak B., *Polska starość*, Gdańsk 2003.

Trivers R. L., *The evolution of reciprocal altruism*, 'Quarterly Review of Biology' 1971, 46, 35–37.

Wiśniewska-Roszkowska K., *Starość jako zadanie*, Warszawa 1989.

Zebrowitz L. A., Montepare J. M., *A social-developmental view of ageism* [in:] T. Nelson (ed.), *Ageism: stereotyping and prejudice against older persons*, Cambridge 2002.

Piotr
Próchniak

Pro-social risk taking and personal values Study of fire-fighters

In our strange days, fire fighting remains a heroic and noble profession. The work is intense, both physically and emotionally. Hazards of this work involve extreme risk from exposure to flames and smoke. To help other people, fire-fighters not avoid situations in which their own health or life is endangered. There is little of systematic studies of fire-fighters. In this studies psychologists were looking for specific mental profile of this group. In addition, some studies are looking for relation between the personality of the fire-fighters and other psychological variables.

Fannin and Dabbs (2003) using NEO-PI, investigated personality differences of the urban male firefighters and the emergency medical service workers. Firefighters had scored lower on Neuroticism, Openness to Experience and Agreeableness than the emergency medical service workers. This studies are contrary to the searching of Dudek (2001). In this study Openness to Experience appears to be predictive of good fire-fighter performance. Goma-i-Freixanet, Perez and Torrubia (1988) found that Spanish fire-fighters were significantly higher on the some aspects of sensation seeking trait than control group of students. Jachnis (1996) investigated the personality differences between fire-fighters, professional boxers, candidates for the boxing sport and amateur sportsmen. Fire-fighters were more likely to shown a low level of reactivity in compared to the other sportsmen.

Meronek and Tan (2004) using 16PF, investigated relationship between the personality of fire-fighters and job satisfaction. Results indicated that only the Independence scale was significantly related to job satisfaction. Liao, Arvey, Nutting and Butler (2001) using MMPI, investigated relationship between the personality of firefighters and level of injury frequency. Inventory scales, conversion, hysteria, psychopathic deviate and social introversion were correlated with an increased level of injury frequency. Moreover, the psychopathic deviate and schizophrenia scale were predictive for longer leave durations after an injury occurred. In the study of Gohm, Baumann and Sniezek (2001), investigated relationship between the personality of firefighters and cognitive difficulties. The firefighters who clearly interpret their emotions were less likely to have cognitive difficulties.

Relatively less attention were paid to the study of values of firefighters. I think that it will be possible to study personal aspirations and personal values of the firefighters. The study of personal values of firefighters can broaden the knowledge about people who risk their own life for other people.

Values have been defined as

> enduring beliefs that a specific mode of conduct or end-state of existence is personally or socially preferable to an opposite or converse mode of conduct or end-state (Rokeach, 1973, p. 5).

Values are assumed to be central aspects of the self-concept. Schwartz (1992) defines a value as a transsituational goal that varies in importance as a guiding principle in one's life. For Schwartz values make up a cognitive representation of challenges, which individual would undertake to survive biologically, to function best in the group as well as to have a satisfying life (Schwartz, 1992; Schwartz, Sagiv, Boehenke, 2000). Some values are very important for the subject, while others are less important. They represent stable but sensible preferences. Values determine impact behavior in personal life and work place (Schwartz, 1999; Ros, Schwartz, Surkiss, 1999).

Ten different value types, each characterized by its own motivational goal, Schwartz (1992) identified: Achievement: personal success and demonstration of competence according to social standards; Power: control or dominance over people, attainment of social status and prestige, Stimulation: excitement, risk taking, novelty, challenge in life; Hedonism: pleasure and sensuous gratification; Self-Direction: independent thought and action; Benevolence: concern for the helping of others in everyday interaction; Conformity: restraint of actions, inclination, and impulses likely to upset or harm others and violate social expectations or norms; Security: safety, stability of society; Tradition: respect, commitment and acceptance of ideas that one's culture impose on the individual; Universalism: tolerance, and protection for the welfare of all people and for nature. These 10 value types were measured using the Schwartz Value Survey, an instrument.

Different combinations and hierarchies of the values represented in Schwartz's theory motivate behavior for different reasons, and guide behavior differently. The particular categories of values create so called 'meta-categories', which may to be introduced in two dimensions. There are following poles of these dimensions:

1) self-oriented (Self-enhancement/Openness to change),

2) other-oriented (Self-transcendence/Conservation).

They can be grouped into four meta-categories, which include the following groups of values:

a) Self-Transcendence: Universalism and Benevolence;

b) Self-enhancement: Hedonism, Achievement, Power;

c) Openness to change: Stimulation, Self-Direction;

d) Conservation: Security, Conformity, Tradition.

Until now, there is no research on the values of firefighters from the Model of Values proposed by S. Schwartz (1992). The purpose of this study was to compare firefighters and control group`s personal values manifested in The Schwartz Model. As discussed earlier, findings in this area prove specific traits of firefighters (Dudek, 2001; Goma-i-Freixanet, Perez, Torrubia, 1988; Jachnis, 1996). Based on The Schwartz Model of Value it was hypothesized that firefighters would score higher on Stimulation Value and Openness to change meta-category than low risk job group.

Method

Participants

The total sample was made up of two groups. The first group consisted of 60 firefighters participated in this study, only men (M = 36,7; SD = 7,6). The mean years of work experience was 10.

The second group was the child, family and school social workers group of 64 men (M = 32,5; SD = 6,6). They were people conducting social work without a particular risk taking in job. In this group 100% individuals had never participated in any high-risk activity. The mean years of work experience was 8.

Procedure

The groups of participants were compared for mean scores on personal values from The Schwartz Model using questionnaire described in the Questionnaire section.

Each of the studied group was informed generally about the goals of the research. Participation in the study was voluntary. Volunteers first had to answer several questions regarding age, sex, and length of experience in job. Child, family and school social workers group was also asked about experience in risky activity. Participants filled in the questionnaire individually, often at home and returned the questionnaire to the author. The questionnaire took less than half an hour.

Questionnaire

In the present study the Schwartz Survey Instrument was used. This questionnaire allows to measure the values as goals in the frameworks of Schwartz theory. The questionnaire consists of a list of 57 values, which are connected with individual or group goals. These values were grouped into 10 categories. The participants have to estimate the values as 'driving life values' according to eight-level scale form – 1 to 7. The level – 1 means that presented value is opposite to participant's principles, 0 – given value is not important for participant, 3 – that value is important for participant, 6 – that value is very important; 7 – given value is the most important one in participant's life.

The coefficient of preference of given category or meta-category is counted as a numerical average of values from particular category or meta-category chosen by participant.

Results

First, the differences in 10 categories of values between firefighters group and control group were studied. The results are presented in table 1.

Table 1. Personal values of the firefighters group and the control group, Student test (t)

Personal values	Firefighters		Control Group		t Student
	M	SD	M	SD	
Power	3,61	1,22	3,43	1,30	0,71
Achievement	4,39	0,90	4,30	1,06	0,48
Hedonism	4,31	1,14	3,64	1,35	2,76**
Stimulation	4,66	1,11	3,40	1,16	5,72***
Self-Direction	5,01	0,70	4,65	0,87	2,37*
Universalism	4,85	1,02	4,65	0,94	0,80
Benevolence	5,20	0,85	4,93	0,86	1,63
Tradition	4,22	1,18	3,92	1,04	0,17
Conformity	5,34	0,85	4,73	1,06	3,12**
Security	5,13	0,86	4,69	0,86	2,22*

$^*\,p < 0{,}05$; $^{**}\,p < 0{,}01$; $^{***}\,p < 0{,}001$.

Firefighters were characterized with significantly higher results in comparison to control group in such scales as: Stimulation ($p < 0{,}01$), Hedonism ($p < 0{,}01$), Self-Direction ($p < 0{,}05$), Conformity ($p < 0{,}01$) and Security ($p < 0{,}05$).

As it was mentioned by Schwartz (1992) different combinations and hierarchies of the values motivate behavior for different reasons, and guide behavior differently. The particular categories of values create so called 'meta-categories'. That is why in our study the differences in the meta-categories of values between firefighters group and control group were studied. The results are presented in table 2.

Table 2. Meta-categories of values of the firefighters and the control group, Student test (*t*)

Meta-categories of values	Firefighters		Control Group		*t* Student
	M	SD	M	SD	
Self-Enhancement	4,10	0,87	3,79	1,03	1,68
Openness to change	4,83	0,74	4,02	0,83	5,31**
Self-Transcendence	5,03	0,87	4,75	0,85	1,47
Conservation	4,88	0,87	4,22	1,07	2,49*

$^* p < 0,05; ^{**} p < 0,01.$

Firefighters were characterized with significantly higher results in comparison to control group in meta-categories: Openness to change ($p < 0,01$) and Conservation ($p < 0,05$).

Discussion

The obtained results show that personal values of the firefighters differ from the personal values of the control group. According to Schwartz (1999), values system impact on attitudes and behavior in work place. The intensity of particular values informs about person's goals of concrete job.

It was found out that firefighters estimated the value Stimulation, Hedonism and meta-category Openness to change higher in comparison to the control group. The hypothesis has been confirmed. Our results found a conformation in the previous studies of sensation seeking of firefighters (Goma-i-Freixanet, Perez, Torrubia, 1988). The obtained results indicate that firefighters are people who appreciate challenges, seek experiences and adventure in their work and like a varied lifestyle. They prefer unforeseeable situations as well as have a tendency to change. The results suggest that firefighters are interested in a broad range of thrill-seeking tasks that provide new experience. What is more, risky situations which are connected with saving other people may be a source of exciting experiences for them. The group of control group does not associate helping others with the search for exciting situations.

On the one hand, in comparison to control group firefighters have higher results in such value as: Stimulation and Hedonism. Unexpectedly, on the other hand, in comparison to control group firefighters have also higher results in such values as: Conformity and Security and meta-categories: Openness to change and Conservation. Conformity reflects the need to restrain inclinations and impulses that disrupt society and therefore represent goals of obedience and self-discipline. Security reflects the need to feel safe through harmony of society. The obtained results indicate that firefighters are people who are not impulsive, self-discipline and able to obey the social norms. They want to reinforce public stability and security too.

Schwartz (1992) identified three main conflicts within this value structure. The first is a conflict between Openness to change and Conservation, the second is a conflict between Self-enhancement and Self-transcendence, the third is a conflict between values referring to the gratification of one's desires (Hedonism) and the acceptance of external limits (Tradition, Conformity). In our study, the firefighters had higher scores in the Stimulation, Hedonism and Conformity. It means that the firefighters have conflict in their value structure. Probably, this conflict can be interpreting from perspective of job of the firefighters. In this job – stability, certainty, security and social order – are very important. The firefighters must often take risk to achieve these values.

References

Dudek B., *Application of the Big Five model for the purpose of selection in fire Services*, „Przeglad Psychologiczny" 2001, 44(4), 495–508.

Fannin N., Dabbs J. M., *Testosterone and the work of firefighters: Fighting fires and delivering medical care*, 'Journal of Research of Personality' 2003, 35, 388–399.

Gohm C. L., Baumann M. R., Sniezek J. A., *Personality in extreme situations: Thinking (or not) under acute stress*, 'Journal of Research in Personality' 2001, 35, 388–399.

Goma-i-Freixanet M., Perez J., Torrubia R., *Personality variables in antisocial and prosocial disinhibitory behavior* [in:] T. E. Moffiitt, S. A. Mednick (ed.), *Biological contributions to crime causation*, Dordrecht 1988.

Jachnis A., *Temperamental antecedents of efficiency of fireman and sportsmen*, „Przeglad Psychologiczny" 1996, 39(1–2), 115–125.

Liao J., Arvey R. D., Nutting S. M., Butler R. J., *Correlates of work injury frequency and during among firefighters*, 'Journal of Occupational Health Psychology' 2001, 6(3), 229–242.

Meronek S. J., Tan J. A., *Personality predictors of firefighter job performance and job satisfaction*, 'Validity Study Applied H.R.M. Research' 2004, 9(1), 39–40.

Rokeach M., *The nature of human values*, New York 1973.

Ros M., Schwartz S. H., Surkiss S., *Basic individual values, work values, and the meaning of work*, 'Applied Psychology: An International Review' 1999, 48(1), 49–71.

Schwartz S. H., *A theory of cultural values and some implications for work*, 'Applied Psychology: An International Review' 1999, 48(1), 23–47.

Schwartz S. H., *Universals in the content and structure of values: Theoretical advances and empirical tests in 20 countries* [in:] M. P. Zanna (ed.), *Advances in experimental social psychology*, 25, 1–65, New York 1992.

Schwartz S. H., Sagiv L., Boehenke K., *Worries and values*, 'Journal of Personality' 2000, 68(2), 309–346.

Piotr
Próchniak

Time perspective of pro- and antisocial risk takers Comparative study of policemen and criminals

Physical-risk taking activities can be classified along a continuum ranging from prosociality to antisociality (e.g. firefighters, policemen – criminals) (Goma-i-Freixanet, 1995). Research concerning physical risk taking behavior have a long tradition in psychological literature. The most widely known research on risk taking behavior is Zuckerman`s work on personality trait sensation seeking. Sensation Seeking trait was defined as:

> the seeking of varied, novel, complex, and intense sensations and experiences, and the willingness to take physical, social, legal, and financial risks for the sake of such experience (Zuckerman, 1994, p. 27).

Research on sensation seeking has been shown to correlate prosocial risk jobs (policemen) or antisocial behavior (criminals) (*ibidem*).

The studies of risk takers personality involved not only sensation seeking trait. Several studies analyzed some other specific traits that correlate to risk taking behavior. For example – short time perspective can correlate to risk taking behavior, what is suggested by research made on people who take up different forms of risky activity e.g. the research concerning people who are addicted to stimulants or who are inclined to take up a risky vehicle driving (Keough, Zimbardo, Boyd, 1999).

Research on sensation seeking suggest that sensation seeking of pro- and antisocial risk takers is very similar (Levin, Brown, 1975; Goma-i-Freixanet, 1995). In this context there is an interesting question: Is time perspective of pro- and antisocial risk takers very similar too? So, the aim of this research is to compartive time perspective of pro- and antisocial risk takers: policemen and criminals.

Time perspective

Realization of the goals, which are hesitant and which are connected with the possibility of failure, goes along with the time perspective, presented on the line: past-present-future. Time presents inner, hidden dimension of personal activity. Analysis of person's time perspective can be an important source of knowledge about human activity, including also about the risky activity.

Research concerning temporal perspective have developed into various directions and planes (Lens, Moreas, 1994; Keough, Zimbardo, Boyd, 1999). Nuttin and Lens (1985) claim that temporal perspective constitutes some mental construct that enables a person to refer to his own past, present, and future. This reference is manifested in the ability to distance oneself from experiences of the past and anticipation of achieving future goals (Nuttin, 1984). Lens and Moreas define the temporal horizon as a part of an individual`s psychological sphere. According Zimbardo and Boyd (1999) the temporal perspective is a multi-dimensional construct connected with an ability to anticipate future events from present perspective. Block (1990) claims that time perspective describes the way people refer to their own past, present and future.

Time perspective has been studied in psychology as a both a personality characteristic and as a cognitive function. As a personality, time perspective is viewed as a stable trait, from the cognitive perspective time perspective is a mental process that involving expectancy and learning (Tobacyk, Nagot, 1994; Zaleski, 1994). In this article time perspective is a combination of a personality characteristic and cognitive dimension.

The past, present and future is part of an individual psychological life space. Some people are past concentrated. Their present and future do not belong to their psychological world. They are only absorbed by the past events. Concentration on the present can be characterized primarily by reducing the temporal horizon to here and now. Present-oriented people are completely absorbed by the present and they do not take into account the future consequences of actually behavior. Whereas concentration on the future can be characterized by determining goals for the more distant perspective. Future-oriented people are absorbed by the future and everything they are doing now is in the service of their future (Lens, Moreas, 1994).

Research of people who take up risky activities are comparatively sparse. In the research by Zimbardo and his associates (1997, 1999) the present time perspective constituted an important predictor of fast vehicle driving and using stimulants, the prospective perspective was negatively correlated with the inclination to the engage in risky behavior. Robbins and Bryan (2004) came to a similar conclusions: young people with longer time perspectives and with a positive attitudes to the future revealed less interest in using drugs or drinking alcohol. Likewise, Agnew and Loving (1998) found that men with a longer time perspectives demonstrated a positive attitudes towards using contraceptives. According to these studies, a hypothesis was formulated that a policemen would score higher on future perspective than the criminals group and similar on presents perspective in comparison to the criminals group.

Method

Participants

The total sample was made up of two groups. A group of policemen who were the participants of a special training preparing them for the peace mission in Kosovo took part in this study. The policemen group consisted of 89 policemen, male only (Mage = 33,1; SD = 4,7). The mean years of work experience was 9. The special course took place at the Police School in Slupsk, Poland. Among the participants there were antiterrorists, pyrotechnics and detectives from the Central Bureau of Investigation (Polish FBI). Participation in the course was voluntary.

The second group was the criminals-prisoners group. This sample consisted of 75 antisocial risk takers incarcerated for having committed armed robbery (Mage = 30,7; SD = 10,1). The mean years of length of punishment was 6 years.

Procedure

Policemen or prisoners was generally informed about the goals of the research. Each participant first had to answer several questions regarding age, sex, and the years of job experience (policemen) and length of punishment (prisoners).

The study of policemen was conducted during the training course at the Police School in Slupsk (Poland) in the Police School's classrooms. Participants answered the questionnaire questions in groups of 20 to 30 people. After the introduction to the study goal and giving instructions about the questionnaire, the policemen individually filled in the questionnaire.

Participants from the criminals group filled in the questionnaire individually at prison and returned the questionnaire to the author.

Questionnaire

In the present study Time Perspective Questionnaire of own authorship was used. The questionnaire included two subscales, which investigated concentration on the present and concentration on the future. Example of present item scale include: 'Present day is most important for me'. The future subscale include such question as, e.g.: 'I have long-term goals'. Particular sentences included in this questionnaire were evaluated by means of the 5-degree Likert scale (1-Strongly disagree; 5-Strongly agree). The questionnaire included 16 statements, eight statements for each subscale. Varimax rotation was performed to assess the factorial structure of the questionnaire. The reliability of the subscale which measured concentration on the present equals Cronbach α = 0,82 reliability of a subscale which measured concentration on future equals Cronbach α = 0,74. Reliability of test-retest after four weeks for the scale of concentration on the present equaled 0,78 whereas for the scale of concentration on the future 0,73.

Results

There were examined the presumptive differences between policemen, criminals in the scope of the present and future time perspective. The results are shown in the table 1 below.

Table 1. Time perspective of policemen and criminals; test Student (t)

Time perspective	Policemen		Criminals		t
	M	SD	M	SD	
Concentration on the present	3,05	0,40	3,36	0,57	−2,33*
Concentration on the future	3,29	0,35	3,15	0,31	1,59

$^*p < 0,01$

Criminals received higher results in the scale of concentration on the present in comparison with policemen (p< 0,01). The future perspective does not differentiates the examined groups.

Discussion

Tests which were carried out aimed at identifying the time perspective of people who undertake a pro-social and antisocial risk activities. Received results of own research show that only one dimension of time perspective distinguishes studied people. The examined policemen have obtained lower results in the concentration on the present in comparison with criminals. In this regard, the hypothesis has been not confirmed. Received results are not similar to those which were received by Agnew and Loving (1998), Robbins and Bryan (2004) or Zimbardo, Keough and Boyd (1997). In these research, all risk takers concentrated more often on the dimension of the present. In this study only criminals concentrated more often on the present. Policemen also took high risk but they are concentrated on the future frequently than on the present.

Before the study it was also assumed that the pro-social daredevils (policemen) and criminals would be characterized by a similar present perspective. Unexpectedly, this assumption has not found a confirmation in the study. From what factors may the different result in the intensity of time perspective of prosocial risk takers (policemen) in comparison with previous studies result? In previous studies the present time perspective constituted an important predictor of risk taking for hedonistic goals (Keough, Zimbardo, Boyd, 1999). Hedonistic risk takers also prefer immediate benefits and it is more difficult for them to postpone getting an award. Probably, the examined policemen are taking risk for other goals than hedonism. Risk taking in policemen work has most often instrumental character. In this job such goals, as: stability, certainty, security and social order – are very important. The policemen must often take risk to achieve these goals but these goals are usually located in the future.

Higher score on present perspective of criminals can be effect of current situation at prison. As a result of social isolation, life of criminals is concentrated on current events, without running away to the future. The future behind the bars for these criminals is very distant (particularly for prisoners sentenced to long-term imprisonment).

In our strange days many people are looking for fast pleasure. So, they take risk: use drugs, drink, make unsafe sex and sometimes kill others. The present is most important for them. On the other hand, there are people who believe that our life is not only here and now. Future is more important than present. So, for better individual and societal future they risk their own life...

References

Agnew Ch. R., Loving T. J., *Future time orientation and condom use attitudes, intentions, and behaviour,* 'Journal of Social Behavior and Personality' 1998, 13(4), 755–764.

Block R. A., *Models of psychological time* [in:] R. A. Block (ed.), *Cognitive models of psychological time,* Hillsdale 1990.

Goma-i-Freixanet M., *Prosocial and antisocial aspects of personality,* 'Personality and Individual Differences' 1995, 19, 125–134.

Keough K. A., Zimbardo P. G., Boyd J. N., *Who's smoking, drinking, and using drugs? Time perspective as predictor of substance use,* 'Basic and Applied Social Psychology' 1999, 21(2), 149–164.

Lens W., Moreas M. A., *Future time perspective: An individual and societal approach* [in:] Z. Zaleski (ed.), P*sychology of future orientation*, Lublin 1994.

Levin B. H., Brown W. E., *Susceptibility to boredom of jailers and low enforcement Officers*, 'Psychological Reports' 1975, 36, 190.

Nuttin J., *Motivation, planning and action (A relational Theory of Behavior Dynamics)*, Leuven 1984.

Nuttin J., Lens W., *Future time perspective and motivation: Theory and research method*, Leuven 1985.

Robbins R. N., Bryan A., *Relationships between future orientation, impulsive sensation seeking, and risk behavior among adjudicated adolescents*, 'Journal of Adolescent Research' 2004, 19, 428–445.

Tobacyk J., Nago E., *Cognitive dimensions used in the prediction of future* [in:] Z. Zaleski (ed.), *Psychology of future orientation*, Lublin 1994.

Zaleski Z., *Toward a psychology of the personal future* [in:] Z. Zaleski (ed.), *Psychology of future orientation*, Lublin 1994.

Zimbardo P. G., Boyd J. N., *Putting time in perspective: A valid reliable individual differences metric*, 'Journal of Personality and Social Psychology' 1999, 77, 1271–1288.

Zimbardo P. G., Keough K. A., Boyd J. N., *Present time perspective as a predictor of risky driving*, 'Personality and Individual Differences' 1997, 23(6), 1007–1023.

Zuckerman M., *Behavioral expressions and biosocial bases of sensation seeking*, New York 1994.

Anetta
Jaworska

In search
of effective rehabilitation
in penal institutions

The pedagogical suggestions presented in this article include the practical social rehabilitation procedures, from openness to the reality's multiplicity perspective, and are directed at all those theoreticians and practicians who are ready to exploit so far unknown possibilities of creating a new identity for the pupil. The suggested methods discussed here do not constitute independent social rehabilitation methods, but are meant to supplement the social rehabilitation methodology through supportive actions. What is vital for social rehabilitation methodology is a generation of approaches synthesizing various methods of interactions and overcoming the limitations of partial paradigms, which are in force while working with socially maladjusted individuals (Konopczyński, 2006; Alderman, 2003; Coyle, 1994).

The task of social rehabilitation children, young people, as well as adult criminal perpetrators incarcerated in penitentiaries in Poland and other post-communist countries is met by many obstacles, connected with infrastructure, financial and personal issues. However, it must be remembered that the decisive role in this area is played by the professional and personal competence of the people undertaking social rehabilitation, both in the open environment as well as in penitentiaries. We may of course contribute to the flow of complaints and criticism concerning jurisdiction, a sense of security with regard to the increasing crime rate and the social rehabilitation ineffectiveness in institutional conditions. On the other hand, we can abandon stagnation and complaining, and concentrate on devising some concept of sensible and creative action in the surrounding reality, which is unlikely to undergo any significant change for a long time. Because of the limited character of this work it will present only a fragment of the research focusing on the sense behind taking empirically unverified action supporting the social rehabilitation process.

The cognitive – behavioral approach, which is currently applied in social rehabilitation, focuses solely on people's individual and external transformations, at the same time considering other aspects of human existence unimportant

(Frindship and others, 2003). This results in narrowing the essence of humanity to the individual and merely external dimension. However, people always function within a given social context, and thus their actions always need to be considered from a collective perspective, through group processes, which can be studied objectively, yet still leaving us with only the external, though this time collective, transformations. We still lack the internal human dimension, which belongs to the realm of introspective sciences, focusing on people's intentions and internal experience, which is becoming an increasingly frequent area of serious scientific research (Jaworska, 2007; Jaworska, 2008). Although the therapy in question should be placed within the scope of introspective interaction, its effects go far beyond the internal human dimension, and that is why I have also included behavioral and social changes in the study. These phenomena are mutually related. Supporting this approach is the nowadays obvious fact, that there exists a correlation between the human mental and physical sphere (e.g. changes in the mental processes are observed in the form of biochemical changes). Such a correlation exists also between an individual isolated from a society and that very society. Thus social order (culture and society) has an influence on the individual, which has already been studied and documented in social rehabilitation pedagogy.

The application base of the discussed method is comprised by generally known and accepted methodical strategies of penitentiary work, while the imperative behind the application of unconventional methods of working with convicts is obeying the rules, methods and directives of resocialization education.

Method

Design and Procedure

The studies on the social rehabilitation effectiveness (concerning personality changes) of breath therapy in penitentiaries was conducted in the form of a research experiment, which took place between January 2006 and June 2007 in three Polish penitentiaries (located in Wierzchowo Pomorskie, Wołowo and Włocławek).

The projecting aim was to search for an optimal social and individual perspective as to life-normalization for people serving a term in prison and directing social rehabilitation action towards achieving inner harmony and a hope of gaining an opportunity to live a worthy life.

The character of the conducted research required a specific methodological approach, including, among others, the necessity to create a set of own research tools. One of the reasons behind creating own tools was the need to obtain such data that would be specific exclusively to the penitentiary environment, i.e. that would provide an image of the way in which those serving a prison sentence perceive themselves, their lives and interpersonal contacts, through the prism of being kept in a penitentiary, and that would relate to reflections and attitudes towards one's own criminal activities, as well as the emotions and motivation connected with them. In the research presented in this work will include only a description of the Inner Self-Attribution Scale, the purpose of which is to determine the prisoners' level of self-awareness and self-perception, in the cognitive, affective and motivational dimension.

Materials

The scale was constructed on the basis of theoretical conditions, and the first criterion used in the selection of the statements used in the scale was their face validity. The scale consists of 24 statements and its internal consistency amounts to Cronbach's alfa – 0,85. The questionnaire consists of 24 statements concerning self-image in the scope of the physical, social, intellectual and moral domain. The respondent can obtain from 2 to 10 points within the scope of each questionnaire component. The lower the score obtained in the scale, the higher the self-esteem regarding the domain in question.

Among the analyzed self-esteem domains we find (Oleś, 2005):

1. The material domain, in the scope of which we analyze:
    a) the cognitive component – the assessment of one's outside appearance;
    b) the affective component – the assessment of one's own physical and material attractiveness through the prism of other people (the most beneficial result being the middle – I am as attractive as others);
    c) the motivational component (searching for the 'I') – aspiring towards a good appearance and material success.

2. The social domain:
    a) the cognitive component – the assessment of how we are perceived by others ('we are what we believe others think we are');
    b) the affective component – self-assessment through the prism of other people (am I better than others) – the middle marks the optimal result;
    c) the motivational component – the need of being accepted by others and of social acclaim.

3. The intellectual domain:
    a) the cognitive component – the assessment of one's own intellectual abilities;
    b) the affective component – the assessment of one's own intellectual abilities through the prism of other people;
    c) the motivational component – striving towards increasing one's intellectual competence.

4. The moral domain:
   a) the cognitive component – the assessment of one's own moral competence ('we are what we think we are');
   b) the affective component – the assessment of one's own morality through
   the prism of other people – average is a good result;
   c) the motivational component – striving towards increasing one's moral
   competence.

Participants

Studies on the accuracy of the constructed scales were conduct-
ed using the reassessment technique on a group of 72 convicts in a penitentiary in
Siedlce. The assessment was conducted twice with a three-week interval.

In the initial phase of the research its scope encompassed a much larger
number of penitentiaries, however the control measurements of the effectiveness of the chosen method were conducted only in those penitentiaries, where it
was possible to continue the experiment for a six month period. Yet we need to
emphasise the significant involvement and support for the research on the part
of the penitentiary officers, who engaged themselves in the research activities
personally and beyond their duties.

During the 16-month analysis period 267 convicts, from the above mentioned penitentiaries, took part in the courses. Some of them were transported to
other facilities during the experiment, released from the penitentiary or resigned
from attending the groups. The control group was formed in a non-biased way,
however, preserving its similarity with respect to mediating variables (age, education, type of crime committed, previous penality, length of sentence) to the
group taking part in the program. In total 236 convicts completed the experiment, while out of the initial 260 people, 249 convicts remained. Participation in
the experiment was completely voluntary, while the trial selection criterion was
the type of crime committed and the length of sentence. For the purpose of the
analysis a group of men aged between 25 and 48 years, convicted to 2 to 10 years
of imprisonment for offences against property as well as against life and health,
was singled out. Pre-test results indicated a lack of significant statistical differences regarding all the studied mediating variables.

The course, the essence of which is constituted by rhythmic breathing (based
on the principles of yoga), was each time carried out for a period of 8 days in the
amount of approximately 20 hours (Jurkonis, 2006). During this time the convicts were becoming familiar with breathing techniques, striving towards deep
body relaxation and emotion relief (pranayama, bhastrika and ujajh breathing)
and learned the basic yoga positions (asan). The aim of the exercises and the
highest level of knowledge concerning conscious breathing is the process called
Sudarshan Krija (SK), which allows total relief and deep relaxation. In this proc-

ess a special role is assigned to the rhythm and continuity of the breath, which is under conscious control for 40 minutes. Each time the breath exercises are combined with static physical exercises, concentrating mostly on stretching the body, and based on katha yoga, as well as with deep relaxation. The aim of the course is to teach the participants (in case of penitentiaries mostly the convicts, but with penitentiary officers as well) the independent performing of simple, static stretching exercises and basic breathing techniques, in order to reduce tension and provide insight into oneself, as well as to teach the ability to overcome negative emotions and gain control over one's own behavior.

After completing the course further experimental work consisted in daily, independent practice by the convicts of the breathing techniques combined with static yoga positions taught to them. What is more, the convicts met two – three times a week for 1,5 hour group exercises in the gymnasium. Each group would voluntarily select a leader who presided over the exercises. In those penitentiaries, where the kindness and involvement of the personnel enabled the convicts regular exercise performance, a post-test was conducted after a period of six months.

Results

Because of the limited character of this work the analysis is merely an introduction to the attempt of describing the phenomena taking place on the deepest levels of human identity, which are hardly attainable to the rules of scientific cognition.

The purpose of the study on self-attribution was to find an answer to the following question:
- in the cognitive domain – what is the level of sympathy or antipathy, as well as respect or hatred towards oneself, in various aspects of human existence.

Moreover the objective of the scientific inquiry is to find answers to these questions:
- in the affective domain – how do people perceive themselves through the prism of those around them;
- in the motivational domain – how do people strive to improve their image in their own eyes: making themselves more attractive, increasing intellectual competence, moral development, as well as acceptance and social acclaim.

Therefore, in my research, I strived not towards the instrumental treatment of self-acceptance, but instead treated it as a conscious attitude towards oneself, which becomes an object of reflection for a person (Tice, 1992). Self-acceptance is an important and inalienable element of knowledge about oneself. The connection between self-acceptance and accepting other people is unquestionable, which is why all attempts of receiving adequate judgment foster an improvement in human interactions. Lower self-esteem – a sense of inferiority – is, according to the psychodynamic approach, one of the causes of anti-social behavior. Only a person who can love and respect him or herself, can love and respect another person. Lack of self-respect leads, in most cases, to destructive or self-destructive behaviors. Helping to regain one's self-respect is the right path in the process leading towards real changes. Even more problematic are the psycho-correctional capabilities of criminals with higher self-esteem, who in most cases display an absolute lack of motivation to work on themselves. So far behavioral therapy has been considered the only relatively effective tool, however, its effects are unusually short-lived.

Presented below are only the results of the retest, conducted after a six-month period of interactions both in the experimental and control group. However, it needs to be emphasized at this point, that in the course of the study, requirements for correct experimental measurements have been met. I shall only mention that the results of the pre-test, distributed before the course, in both convict groups (experimental and control) did not differ in a statistically significant way, while the results of the experimental group – before and after the experiment – displayed significant statistical differences in the domains presented below. Therefore, the changes described below can be attributed, with all responsibility to the introduction of the experimental factor.

Self-esteem contains at least three domains, in the scope of which an individual can assess him or herself, i.e. the material, social and mental (intellectual and moral) domain. One can also speak of a certain hierarchy of various forms or domains of the self-image the, e.g. a person can value his or her material aspect more, by considering his or her looks and life-comfort more valuable than the mental disposition or other people's regard. This self-assessment, as a set of one's detailed assessments, leads, in consequence, to formulating a generalized self-image and includes both cognitive and emotional aspects.

In the course of the conducted research particular relationships between systematic yoga practice, taught during the course, and changing one's self-esteem were noted. However, as the results presented in tables 1, 2 and 3 indicate, these changes do not include all the self-attribution domains in a statistically significant way.

Because of the lack of significant statistical differences with respect to self-perception in the physical domain, it was decided to disregard this domain in the following interpretation. Thus we need to draw the conclusion that there is no influence of the conducted breath-therapy on the convicts' self-esteem, connected with their physical domain (looks and outside appearance).

On the other hand high statistical significance was noticed regarding the changes in the area the convicts' social functioning domain, or more precisely, its motivational part. After a six-month period of therapy, self-esteem, in the scope of the social-scale motivational component, equaled 3,65 (the lower the score the higher the self-esteem) while in the control group the result showed no significant change and equaled 4,29 (see table 1). Thus the role of the exercises, in this situation, consisted in intensifying the need of social approval in the freeman environment, which should be regarded as a significant element supporting the social rehabilitation process. The therapy brought no statistically measurable changes in self-perception, in the area of other social domain components.

Table 1. Self-attribution in the scope of the social domain

Domain	Social domain					
Component	Cognitive		Affective		Motivational	
Group	n E.	n C.	n E.	n C.	n E.	n C.
	236	249	236	249	236	249
M	5,47	5,63	4,25	4,41	3,65	4,29
SD	1,61	1,59	1,48	1,32	2,08	1,40
Student's *t* result	−1,03		−1,25		−3,92	
Significance level	ni		ni		$p < 0,001$	

Note. The following notations are applied in the tables: M (statistical mean), SD (standard deviation), E (experimental group), C (control group).

After the experiment statistically significant differences in the experimental and control group, also in the area of the intellectual domain, occurred only in the motivational part. The mean result achieved by the people taking part in systematic breathing-therapy exercise after six months equaled 3,33, while the group which did not attend the sessions this result stayed on the level of 5,14 (see table 2), from which we can draw the conclusion that during the sessions people developed motivation to raise their intellectual competence and ability development. It appears that the reasons for this need to be sought in the general increase of motivation to change one's life.

Table 2. Self-attribution in the scope of the intellectual domain

Domain	Intellectual domain					
Component	Cognitive		Affective		Motivational	
Group	n E.	n C.	n E.	n C.	n E.	n C.
	236	249	236	249	236	249
M	5,19	5,14	6,62	6,70	3,33	5,14
SD	1,51	1,70	1,07	1,15	1,53	1,23
Student's *t* result	0,32		−1,74		14,06	
Significance level	ni		ni		$p < 0,001$	

The results in table 3 present the results of the retest concerning the moral domain. Significant differences in self-attribution in the moral domain, in the scope of all its components, have been noted in both groups. In the cognitive domain the group attending breath-therapy obtained an average result of 5,47. The control group's result equaled 4,11. Thus in this case positive self-esteem connected with the moral domain was lower for those people who attended the breathing-therapy, than for the convicts who did not. As it appears this result can be related with the development of self-consciousness and a feeling of guilt for one's action. High self-esteem in the moral domain in the case of the convicts from the control-group (the feeling of being conscientious and honest) is rather an effect of using defense mechanisms. Self-evaluation of one's own morality, after six months of exercise, was transformed and became more adequate in relation to reality. In this case a substantial number of convicts, in assessing their moral competence, assumed a tendency to average their results, rather than take their moral perfection for granted. This effect should be considered as one of the most crucial in the presented therapy.

Table 3. Self-attribution in the scope of the moral domain

Domain	Moral domain					
Component	Cognitive		Affective		Motivational	
Group	n E.	n C.	n E.	n C.	n E.	n C.
	236	249	236	249	236	249
M	5,47	4,11	5,93	4,64	3,32	5,21
SD	1,84	1,38	1,20	1,64	1,90	1,85
Student's t Result	9,10		−9,72		13,16	
Significance level	$p < 0,001$		$p < 0,001$		$p < 0,001$	

In the affective domain the convicts who did not take part in the experiment and did not change their assessment from six months before, responded true or definitely true to the question whether they considered themselves better people, who have done less harm in their lives than the other convicts. This tendency was changed in the exercise group, causing significant statistical differences between both groups. This appears to be strongly connected with neutralizing mechanisms (justification) of criminal behaviors, described among others by D. Matz and G. M. Sykes (Pospiszyl, 1998). After six months of yoga training the mean result differences between the groups gained high statistical significance and equaled 5,93 in the experimental group and 4,64 in the control group, which means that those convicts, assessing themselves through the prism of other people serving a term of imprisonment, and who have systematically practiced yoga, began to perceive their own imperfection. What occurred then was a rise of self-consciousness in the moral domain. Without this element, without the ability to perceive one's mistakes aspiring to a change in one's life or to a moral transformation is not possible. This aspiration also took on differences of high statistical significance in the motivational domain. As a result of applying the program there was an increase in the desire to help others and become a better person among the convicts. The experimental group's mean result, 3,32, differs from the result of the group which did not attend breathing exercise, amounting to 5,21. Such a result arrangement indicates a rise of motivation to make changes in the moral dimension in people systematically doing exercise taught during the course.

The consequences of disregarding the external and internal self-consciousness levels lead to the increase in self-deceit and in distortions regarding other people's assessments and opinions. This tendency is especially visible among those prisoners, who blame their current state on life circumstances, an unjust sentence and a negative attitude towards them, as presented by those around them. People deprived of freedom, who are obviously concerned with the inability to satisfy many substantial needs function on a level of defensive self-consciousness, the purpose of which is to retain a positive image of oneself. Only a full development of other personality levels – external, internal and reflexive, can lead to an adequate self-assessment, thus contributing to the emergence of, at least, a desire to make changes within oneself.

Therefore, as long as there is a lack of self-consciousness in all its levels among convicts, social rehabilitation will remain ineffective, because a person with an inadequate self-image will strive to retain that image. The need to retain an inadequate self-image makes following the direction, which the society considers desirable, and the changes, which are in fact positive for the individual, impossible. Therefore, inadequate self-attribution not only prevents personality development, but also contributes to its deterioration. This deterioration in the end leads the convicts to: a further build-up of defense mechanisms, particularly a rationalization of their criminal conduct and sustaining their high opinion of themselves; raising the significance of their doings and past life-choices; attributing their own traits and motives, in accordance with their own reasoning, regarding their conduct; and, what completely thwarts the effectiveness of social rehabilitation, a tendency to being attached to the past lifestyle and resisting changing it.

Alternative methods raise justified controversy, mainly because of the problems with their theoretical interpretation and scientific analysis. However, perhaps it is worth to suspend our fossilized views of the world for the time being, and refrain from taking a stand. Certain astonishment with the eccentricity of a method should not lead to doubt as to the feasibility of our actions, but to discovering the real sense, which goes beyond the accepted obviousness of the outside world.

However, it needs to be strongly emphasized, that although alternative methods of working with prisoners, coupled with an openness to pluralism and full involvement of the penal personnel, may constitute a perfect support to the social rehabilitation process in penitentiaries, they cannot be a substitute to acknowledged forms of penitentiary work (Mathews, Pitts, 1998).

Discussion

In contemporary Polish- and English-language literature we can find very few convincing scientific facts in support of programs focused on the realm of the prisoners' self-reflection and self-consciousness, and based on the changes taking place in the deepest layers of their identity. At the same time, nowadays it is hard to doubt, that effective social rehabilitation cannot be based on the unidimensionality of interactions, while multilayer interventions have become the imperative behind the effective correction of deviating behaviors. Multidimensionality, complexity, heterogeneity are aspects of all contemporary social-reality, which also includes the penitentiary. Worldwide studies on the effectiveness of yoga exercises, and most of all the process called Sudarshan Krija were so far conducted mainly in the scope of preventing depression and eliminating post-traumatic stress disorder. The influence of Sudarshan Krija on cognitive and neuromental problems connected with post-traumatic stress disorder were studied by Sharon Sageman from the New York University in 2001 (Sageman, 2002). The impulse to undertake the study was the terrorist attack on WTC on 11th November 2001. It involved three groups of people with the biggest exposure to stress connected with terrorist attacks: policemen, Wall Street Corporation employees and other members of the New York community. The depression and anxiety level among the WTC employees, measured with the Davidson Trauma Scale, turned out significantly higher than among the general population of the city. They were also more likely to abuse sedatives. The measured symptoms included obsessive-compulsive behavior, somatic symptoms, hostility, signs of paranoia and psychotic symptoms. Thanks to the controlled breathing process, practiced in the Sudarshan Krija, earlier traumatic experience is evoked. Sageman argues that by providing opportunities to relive the emotions and physical symptoms of stress, however this time in a safe amount, these emotions were gradually extinguished and patients began to regain control over them through breathing. Several months of work on breathing contributed to as statistically significant ($p < 0,001$) decrease in stress symptoms connected with anxiety. However, comparing Sageman's results with my studies on the convict population is the most important issue in the present discussion. In this scope we can see a relation between an increase in the correlational approach to stress (significance level equaling $p < 0,05$), indicated by Sageman, and the result obtained by me, indicating an increase in self-attribution in the motivational domain, in the intellectual, social and moral sphere (see table 1, 2, 3).

What is interesting, from the point of view of the possibilities given by yoga practice, in the scope of the effect it has on people deprived of freedom, is the research carried out by Verne Suarez (Suarez, 2002), during the first Sudarshan Krija courses in Lancaster. During the first quarter of 2001 a study was carried out on courses for juvenile delinquents. The study was based on interview questionnaires and on STAI forms (State-Trait Anxiety Inventory created by C. D. Spielberg). The research was carried out on children and young people aged from 13–18 years, who were convicted of violence related crimes (armed robbery, aggravated burglary, murder, rape and extortion). The courses were organized in small groups and were attended by a total of 86 young people (72 completed the experiment), most of whom were Los Angeles juvenile-gang members. The program was carried out for a period of one week, in the amount of approximately 25 hours. After finishing the course the participants would proceed with one hour of meditation and with using breathing techniques, taught during the course, 3 times a week after, following their waking up, for a period of 8 weeks. A study conducted afterwards indicated the following:
– in the realm of subjective feelings – better sleeping, a decrease in emotional excitability (longer reaction time for provocation), a decrease in anger and a general calming down;
– in the STAI scale – a significant fall in state-anxiety (in all courses but one, consisting of four participants), on a statistically significant level $p < 0,004$;
– in the behavioral realm – fights decreased by 38% while disciplinary punishments decreased by 23%.

These are, so far, the only studies in research literature, conducted in penitentiary conditions. Although the dependent variables, defined in the above research, do not constitute equivalents of the variables presented in this work, it is worth to mention the results obtained by Suarez, since the measurements were done among people displaying criminal maladjustment, who were placed in penitentiaries. The results of the Lancaster experiment indicate the usefulness of the applied breathing techniques in the scope of influencing people deprived of freedom.

References

Alderman N., *Contemporary approaches to the management of irritability and aggression following traumatic brain injury*, 'Neuropsychological Rehabilitation' 2003, 211–241.
Coyle A., *The prison we deserve*, Northampton 1994.
Frindship L., Blud L., Travers R., Nugent E., Thornton D., *Accreditation of offending behaviour programs in HM prison service. What works' in practice*, 'Legal and Criminological Psychology' 2003, 4, 68–81.

Jaworska A., *Antystresowa wartość alternatywnej terapii dźwiękiem w zakładzie karnym* [w:] A. Jaworska, Ł. Wirkus, P. Kozłowski (red.), *Psychospołeczne determinanty niedostosowania społecznego oraz nowatorskie prądy działań zaradczych*, Słupsk 2007.

Jaworska A., *Readaptacyjna wartość sztuki w zakładach karnych*, Słupsk 2008.

Jurkonis B., *Przeciwdziałanie agresji i przemocy w zakładach zamkniętych*, Słupsk 2006.

Konopczyński M., *Metody twórczej resocjalizacji*, Warszawa 2006.

Mathews R., Pitts J., *Rehabilitation, recidivism and realism: Evaluating violence reduction programs in prison*, 'Prison Journal' 1998, 98, 390–406.

Oleś P., *Wprowadzenie do psychologii osobowości*, Warszawa 2005.

Pospiszyl K., *Resocjalizacja. Teoretyczne podstawy oraz przykłady programów oddziaływań*, Warszawa 1998.

Sageman S., *How SK can treat the cognitive, psychodynamic, and neuro-psychiatric problems of post traumatic stress disorder. Proceedings of the international symposium on sudarshan kriya, pranayam & consciousness*, New Delhi 2002.

Suarez V., *Anxiety study at lance alternative program. Proceedings of the international symposium on sudarshan kriya, pranayam & consciousness*, New Delhi 2002.

Tice D. M., *Self-concept change and self-presentation the looking glass self is a magnifying glass*, 'Journal of Personality and Social Psychology' 1992, 63.

9 788375 871883

www.ingramcontent.com/pod-product-compliance
Lightning Source LLC
Chambersburg PA
CBHW050456080326
40788CB00001B/3885